Katrina Nattress

111 Places
in Portland
That You Must
Not Miss

Photographs by Jason Quigley

T0150538

emons:

To Inge, your love of exploration has always inspired me, and your spirit will be felt on every adventure I embark on from here on out.
K. N.

To my family, and my city.
J. Q.

© Emons Verlag GmbH
All rights reserved
All photos © Jason Quigley, except:
Elk Rock Garden (ch. 27): Rachel Holbrook, Head Gardener,
Elk Rock Garden of the Bishop's Close; Portland Gay Men's Chorus
(ch. 83): Image courtesy of the Portland Gay Men's Chorus
Art Credits:
Art Fills the Void! Mural (ch. 3): Frank DeSantis of Gorilla Wallflare
Bonito's Il Femminiello (ch. 12): Giuseppe Bonito
Cleary Sculpture Garden (ch. 20): Sculptor Lee Hunt
The Green Man of Portland (ch. 35): Daniel Duford
Morrison Street Minigallery (ch. 57): Alissa Tran
Portlandia Statue (ch. 87): Sculptor Raymond Kaskey
The Zymoglyphic Museum (ch. 111): Jim Stewart
© Cover motif: shutterstock.com/allegro
Edited by Karen E. Seiger
Layout: Eva Kraskes, based on a design
by Lübbeke | Naumann | Thoben
Maps: altancicek.design, www.altancicek.de
Basic cartographical information from Openstreetmap,
© OpenStreetMap-Mitwirkende, ODbL
Printing and binding: CPI – Clausen & Bosse, Leck
Printed in Germany 2020
ISBN 978-3-7408-0750-4
First edition

Did you enjoy this guidebook? Would you like to see more?
Join us in uncovering new places around the world on:
www.111places.com

Foreword

Portland, you've changed. Traffic's worse than ever, as is the cost of living. High-rise apartment buildings obstruct the East Side skyline. Some neighborhoods are unrecognizable from 10 years ago. The city's too crowded… but I still love you.

The rise in population means people from all walks of life call Portland home, sharing their culture with us. Resilient Portlanders have adopted the "reintrification" mindset of rooting businesses in their gentrified neighborhoods to support their community. Locals champion "Old Portland" institutions to ensure they live on for years to come. In the City of Roses, we have each other's backs, no matter the seismic shift.

In these pages you'll discover new places and activities, from dog tap rooms to bike polo, while gaining new perspective on some of Portland's most iconic landmarks. You'll learn about the city's many superlatives, including the only vegan strip club in the world, the smallest park in the world, the oldest drag queen in the world, and the country's first bridge designed for pedestrians, transit, and cyclist traffic only. You'll be educated on the good, the bad, and the ugly of the city's history – from inspirational suffragettes to shameful segregation laws – and find places that embody the "Make Portland Weird" mantra.

But most importantly, you'll learn the stories of the people behind all these places. You'll meet a Native American, homosexual herbalist. You'll meet businessmen and -women aspiring to shift the cannabis industry from white male dominance. You'll meet the world's first nonprofit pub owner. You'll meet entrepreneurs who strive to make sex toys safe and comfortable for every body. You'll meet the women who opened Portland's first urban winery.

As long as people like these live in the City of Roses, it will be a remarkable place to live and visit. No matter how much it changes.

K. N.

111 Places

1 Abernethy Green

The true end of the Oregon Trail

When George Abernethy came to Oregon in 1840, his influence was immediate. He arrived in the territory aboard a 600-ton, three-masted barkentine called *Lausanne* as part of the Methodists' "Great Reinforcement," a missionary effort to convert the indigenous Pacific Northwest peoples to Christianity. Acting as the financial manager, Abernethy bought out the stores when the mission closed in 1844 and moved them to the territory's center of settlement and trade, Oregon City.

Aside from being an entrepreneur, the New York native was also an insightful politician and became Oregon's first and only provisional governor after winning elections in 1845 and 1847. As Abernethy's power rose in the territory, hundreds of thousands of pioneers were packing up their necessary belongings and heading west in hopes of a better life. While the technical end of the Oregon Trail was the land claim office in downtown Oregon City, those who endured the treacherous 2,170-mile journey often arrived in October and needed a place to camp for the winter. Whether settlers came by raft or Barlow Road, the stopping point was Abernethy Green, George's expansive private land. He and his wife Anna offered encampments to those in need, as his property was more spacious and flat than the land in town. Since he owned the area's only mercantile, the weary travelers became loyal customers.

Today, the End of the Oregon Trail sprawls across that very land Abernethy provided to pioneers. Amongst the interpretive center's many exhibits is a garden that displays a plaque commemorating Abernethy Green. Visitors can also take an interactive look at life on the Trail through artifacts that include a buggy, dress, pitcher, and four pieces of china that survived the Oregon Trail, as well as an exhibit on the region's Native people, provided by the Confederated Tribes of Grand Ronde.

Address 1726 Washington Street, Oregon City, OR 97045, +1 (503) 657-9336, www.historicoregoncity.org | **Getting there** Free parking in on-site lot | **Hours** Mon–Sat 9:30am–5pm, Sun 10:30am–5pm | **Tip** George Abernethy died in 1877, at the age of 70. You can visit his grave at the River View Cemetery (see ch. 91) (300 SW Taylors Ferry Road, www.riverviewcemetery.org).

2 Airplane Home
It's exactly what it sounds like

When you wind up the long, unpaved driveway of 15270 SW Holly Hill Road in rural Hillsboro and come across a Boeing 727 perched neatly in the woods, it feels like you've stumbled across a horror film set or a scene from *Lost*. But you've actually arrived at Bruce Campbell's home.

Campbell recalls seeing his first airliner boneyard at the age of 10, and even as a kid, he thought it was such a waste. In 1999, the retired engineer purchased a retired Olympic jet for $100,000. He had it flown into the Hillsboro Airport and towed through the streets of downtown to his 10-acre plot of land. Though he's owned his Airplane Home for over two decades, Campbell is constantly fixing it up; however, that doesn't hinder him from welcoming visitors and hosting events.

Anyone is welcome to explore the premises without an appointment, and those curious to tour the 727 can schedule with Campbell via email (he even offers free overnight lodging). Before entering the jetliner via air stairs, visitors are required to follow a sterile procedure and leave their shoes behind to ensure no contaminants enter the cabin. Campbell greets his guests at the cabin door, which he describes as a safe – difficult to penetrate and secure enough to make sure the elements stay outside. The living space is modest: the original bathroom is connected to a septic tank, and water comes from a well. His kitchen consists of a microwave and toaster oven, and he built a rudimentary shower. He sleeps on a convertible couch. Original seats line the walls towards the front of the aircraft, and the cockpit is still intact. Campbell also hosts concerts on the wing of the plane and is open to coordinating public and private events with interested parties.

Though his space is very cool, Campbell's real goal is to showcase the practicality of airplane homes in hopes that others will follow in his footsteps.

Address 15270 SW Holly Hill Road, Hillsboro, OR 97123, +1 (503) 628-2936, www.airplanehome.com, bruce@airplanehome.com | **Getting there** Free on-site parking | **Hours** By appointment only | **Tip** If you're an aviation nut, make a day of it and visit the Spruce Goose at the Evergreen Aviation & Space Museum (500 NE Captain Michael King Smith Way, McMinnville, OR 97128, www.evergreenmuseum.org).

3 _Art Fills the Void!_ Mural
Portland's oldest surviving mural

In the 1980s, Portland was a blank canvas for street artists. Its low-lying commercial buildings and abundant wall space made it a haven for mural painters, and vibrant pieces began sprouting up, some illegally.

In 1982, a group of anonymous artists grew tired of staring at a drab wall and painted a giant, bruised banana on the side of a property at the corner of SE 12th and Division. They scrawled the slogan "Art Fills the Void!" in black alongside the fruit and signed their masterpiece "Gorilla Wallflare." The building owner was surprised by the 30 by 50 foot painting but decided not to cover it.

Though the piece looks like an Andy Warhol reference, one of the artists involved said it was originally about the banana republic wars in Central America and was going to say, "Viva Mi Banana." However, the group decided to change the exclamation to protest the dull wall instead. The group would go on to paint two more murals around the city as political statements. After each "attack," they sent typed letters to local officials and news outlets stating their actions and motivation.

Now, _Art Fills the Void!_ is Portland's oldest mural and only "gorilla graffiti" to survive a lengthy legal battle between the city and AK Media over signage rights. In 2015, the Portland Street Art Alliance (PSAA) facilitated the painting's renovation after decades of vandalism and haphazard touch ups, with the help of Gorilla Wallflare's own Frank DeSantis.

"We had a lot of volunteers come out multiple days to help with the mural restoration, even people who lived in the community that we didn't previously know," says PSAA's Tiffany Conklin. "Some of these neighbors now serve as 'local guardians' of the mural, keeping the area clean and notifying us if any damage occurs."

Art Fills the Void! graces the corner of 12th and Division, saving passersby from a dreadfully dull wall indeed.

Address 1125 SE Division Street, Portland, OR 97202, +1 (503) 847-9406, www.pdxstreetart.org, info@pdxstreetart.org | Getting there TriMet to SE Division & 12th (Line 2); MAX to Clinton Street / SE 12th (Orange Line); free street parking | Hours Unrestricted | Tip Walk down the street to marvel at Irish artist Finbar Dac's 70-foot geisha with live plants growing in her hair (959 SE Division Street).

4 Battleship Oregon Memorial

A Spanish-American War hero

How many times have you walked along the Waterfront Park and stopped to explore the Battleship Oregon Memorial? If you're like a lot of Portlanders, the answer is probably "never." The memorial is admittedly small – the salvaged mast of USS *Oregon* surrounded by signage – but the story it tells is an important one in US history.

The steel-armored, 42-gunned ship was completed on October 26, 1893 and was built as a short-distance, sea-going battleship. Three years later it was commissioned, designated as a battleship for the US Navy. It took nearly two more years for the USS *Oregon* to see action, and on March 19, 1898, it was called to service in the Spanish-American War. Stationed in the Pacific Ocean, the ship propelled south, around the horn of South America to fight in the Caribbean Sea. Under the command of Civil War veteran Charles Edgar Clark, the *Oregon* was equipped with 2,000 extra tons of ammunition and coal to prepare for its unprecedentedly long voyage.

The battleship reached its destination of Callao, Peru on May 26, where it joined the North Atlantic Squadron, completing the 14,500-mile journey in just 66 days and exceeding all limitations of a short-distance vessel. During the famed battle of Santiago, amongst other war action, the *Oregon*'s 13-inch guns outmatched its adversaries and became an integral factor in America's victory.

After the war, the *Oregon* saw little action. It was decommissioned in 1903, brought back as a reserve ship in World War I, and retired from service in 1919. For years it floated on Portland's waterfront as a memorial and museum; however, after Pearl Harbor was bombed, the US government tore the ship apart. Now the mast is all that remains, serving as a tribute to the Spanish-American War and all marines who served aboard the mighty *Oregon*.

Address SW Naito Parkway and SW Pine Street, Portland, OR 97204, +1 (503) 823-7529, www.portlandoregon.gov/parks | Getting there TriMet to SW Oak & 1st (Line 16); MAX to SW Oak & 1st (Blue & Red Lines); metered street parking | Hours Unrestricted | Tip If you're fascinated by nautical history, head toward the water from the Battleship Oregon Memorial and visit the Oregon Maritime Museum, which happens to be housed on a historic tugboat (198 SW Naito Parkway, www.oregonmaritimemuseum.org).

5 The Belmont Goats

A community herd

A herd of 14 goats and 1 hen reside at the Carey Boulevard Greenway in North Portland. The sprawling, fenced-in field is prime grazing territory, and wooden structures filled with hay give its residents reprieve from the weather on particularly inclement days. But who are these goats, and how did they get here?

In 2010, landscape architect Brett Milligan suggested an idea to developer Killian Pacific: rent out a herd of goats to clear out the brush surrounding SE Belmont and Taylor Streets and SE 11th and 10th Avenues. Though the advice made sense, Milligan had ulterior motives. He was curious how the community would react to goats living in an urban landscape. To his delight, they embraced their new neighbors with open arms and named the area "Goat Field."

Three years later, a local business owner who helped take care of the rented herd arranged to have his own goats move onto the lot. Where their predecessors were hired out to clear brush in various locations, these animals would be thought of as permanent residents. All was good until an impending development project threatened to split up the herd. Volunteer caretakers stepped up and purchased the goats, creating The Belmont Goats, a nonprofit named for the herd's original home.

The goats have since moved locations a few times, but Chester, Lefty, Carl, Phil, Bailey, Duchess, Dusty, Hickory, Bambi, Cooper, Clover, Precious, Atho, Winter, and Juniper the hen have not been separated. The herd is always visible through the fence, and scheduled public visiting hours allow you to pet, brush, and receive some goat therapy to your heart's content.

A team of volunteers is always on hand to make sure the visit is enjoyable for all parties and answer any questions you may have about the goats. Just make sure to follow the rules posted on the gate, for everyone's sake.

Address 6631 N Syracuse Street, Portland, OR 97203, +1 (971) 301-4628,
www.thebelmontgoats.org, ask@thebelmontgoats.org | Getting there TriMet to N Lombard
& Westanna (Line 75); free street parking on N Macrum Avenue | Hours Sat & Sun
11am–2pm (all ages), Wed 5–7pm (ages 18+ only) | Tip On your way to visit the goats
(and hen), swing by Cathedral Coffee for a nice little pick-me-up to sip while socializing
with the herd (7530 N Willamette Boulevard, www.cathedralcoffee.com).

6__Bible Club

Piss on the Prohibition

Despite its nondescript craftsman-house exterior with a shining green light in the window and era-appropriate, well, everything, Bible Club isn't just another speakeasy – it's a museum you can drink in. In the year and a half that it took for the bar to open its doors, former owner Ryk Maverick scoured the internet and antique stores on multiple continents for pieces. He thumbed through estate sales and swap meets across the globe, meticulously collecting treasures to display in the bar. As a result, nearly every object housed in Bible Club is pre-1930s and American-made, from the crystal glassware and *Repeal 18th Amdt For Prosperity* plate that's tacked behind the sturdy wood bar, to the 24-carat gold-leaf ceiling and 1928 radio, which, of course, plays music from the same time period. Even the screws are era-appropriate flatheads that Maverick compulsively replaced after construction workers initially used Phillips-head ones.

That same love and attention to detail is showcased in every plate of food and cocktail served. You won't find well liquor here. However, along with compassion comes a sense of humor. One of the first pieces your eyes settle on upon entering Bible Club is a scandalous painting of a young nun sprawled on a bed, her habit open to reveal what's underneath. Maverick always considered this the filter: if you get offended by the artwork, you probably shouldn't hang out here.

Though Maverick no longer owns Bible Club, his vision still lives on in every thoughtful detail. You'll notice something different with each visit.

Even the bathrooms come with impeccable attention to detail and tongue-in-cheek décor. Copper tank toilets and turn-of-the-century tiling make for a fascinating trip to the loo. In the men's restroom, you'll even find a *HOOVER* plaque strategically situated as a pee guard, begging patrons to piss on J. Edgar's Prohibition.

Address 6716 SE 16th Avenue, Portland, OR 97202, +1 (971) 279-2198, www.bibleclubpdx.com, bibleclubpdx@gmail.com | Getting there TriMet to SE Milwaukie & Claybourne (Line 19); free street parking | Hours Wed & Thu 5pm–midnight, Fri & Sat 5pm–1am, Sun 4–11pm | Tip For more Prohibition-era imbibing, visit Circa 33 and enter the speakeasy through the bookcase at the back, to the right (3348 SE Belmont Street, www.circa33.com).

7 Bike Farm

A bike shop for DIYers

Portland is known for its cycling community, and bike repair and workshop spaces flourish here. But none are quite like Bike Farm. The name is fitting – as soon as you walk in, your eyes fixate on parts sprouting from the concrete ground and suspending overhead. Loose wheels, handlebars, gears, and frames hang in the warehouse-like space, begging to get picked by their next owner. In the middle of the shop is a workspace inviting you to repair or tune-up your bike in a DIY environment. There's a big, pink mural painted on the wall depicting the anatomy of a bike, which is a helpful reference tool, but if you get stuck, fear not. A number of mechanics are always surveying the floor, ready to help with your project.

Bike Farm is a volunteer-run collective that thrives off donations. Its main model is a membership system ranging from monthly ($20) to lifelong ($200). A membership grants you full access to the shop, professional tools, and mechanic assistance. Non-members are welcome to use the workshop for a $5-per-hour fee; however, Bike Farm does offer free shop time on specific days of the month and is willing to trade volunteer hours for shop time or parts. Above all else, its mission is to create a space for bike safety and education, build community, and promote sustainable transportation no matter your income level.

Aside from providing used parts and a workshop, Bike Farm also sells refurbished bikes that were hand-built using donated pieces, as well as select new parts. If you scour the floor thoroughly enough, you might even find a free bike that needs some tender love and care.

Though Bike Farm is thriving, it's always looking for new volunteers to help with everything from building bikes to washing dishes. If you're interested in becoming part of the team, fill out the volunteer form on Bike Farm's website and attend one of its monthly orientation meetings.

Address 1810 NE 1st Avenue, Portland, OR 97212, +1 (971)533-7428, www.bikefarm.org, bikefarm@bikefarm.org | **Getting there** TriMet to NE Broadway & 2nd (Line 17); Portland Streetcar to NE Broadway & 2nd (B Loop); free street parking | **Hours** Mon & Wed 5–9pm, Fri–Sun noon–4pm | **Tip** If you want to support another bike-centric nonprofit visit Bikes For Humanity PDX (3366 SE Powell Boulevard, www.b4hpdx.org).

8__ Black PNW Collection

Celebrating Black culture in the North Portland Library

On the southwest corner of North Killingsworth Street and Commercial Avenue sits the North Portland branch of the Multnomah County Library system. The brick building has stood tall as a pillar of the Black community since the early 20th century, in a city that continues to struggle with its infamous reputation of lacking diversity.

The library first opened its doors in 1913, and in the 100-plus years that have passed, its devotion to the community is still on full display. Upon entering, the back wall directs eyes to the Black Resources Collection, which includes over 7,000 books, films, periodicals, pieces of music, and other items related to the African-American experience, as well as works created by people of African and African-American descent. Though some pieces are housed in other library branches, most of them live here.

In the summer of 2018, the library launched a new collection that is specific to the North Portland location. The Black Pacific Northwest Collection features literature, film, music, and other items that express the Black experience in the Pacific Northwest. Every piece of work in this tailor-made group was written by or about Black people in Oregon, Washington, Idaho, and Northern California. The ever-growing collection provides accessibility to voices that aren't always heard, represents those who deserve to shine, and puts on display the region's sometimes hard to swallow history.

The library also supports the Black community through its art. On the staircase landing before reaching the second floor, a triptych entitled *Isis* splashes the wall with oranges, purples, and blues. The vibrantly colored fabric painting depicts a Black goddess riding a lizard and was created by the late Charlotte Laverne Lewis – a local artist, loyal to her community, who passed away in 1999 but lives on in her artwork.

Address 512 N Killingsworth Street, Portland, OR 97217, +1 (503) 988-5123, www.multcolib.org/library-location/north-portland, ask-the-library@multco.us | **Getting there** TriMet to N Killingsworth & Vancouver (Line 44); free street parking | **Hours** Mon & Tue noon–8pm, Wed–Sat 10am–6pm, Sun noon–5pm | **Tip** After perusing the library, hop across the street for some mouthwatering oxtail, jerk chicken, and sweet fried plantains at Jamaican Homestyle Cuisine (441 N Killingsworth Street, www.jamaicanhomestylepdx.com).

9 __ Blodgett Family Doll House
A world of childish wonder awaits

The Portland Children's Museum has been piquing youthful curiosity since 1946, making it the oldest museum of its kind west of the Mississippi and the sixth oldest in the world. The 50,000-square-foot building houses exhibits that allow kids to build, play, explore, and learn as they construct their own bridge or shop for groceries at The Market, a children-designed farm-to-table setup, complete with barista station, mushroom log, and food truck (so Portland!).

Though the museum is known for its thoughtfully curated, large-scale exhibits, past the Theater, through the twinkling Twilight Trail, beyond the Maker's Studio, and to the left of the Clay Studio sits an old dollhouse. It's been on display since the museum moved to its current location in 2001, but its relatively small size makes it easy to miss. Peeking through its plexiglass casing, you see the careful detail Forrest and Beverly Blodgett put into creating a piece of art in 1986. Each doll represents a member of their family; miniature prints of real photos line the walls; tiny items fill every closet and cabinet; a fully decorated patio and deck jut out the back, despite not being viewable from the front. Forrest even wired the whole thing with electricity, real light switches and all.

When Beverly passed away, the family thought it would be unfair for one kid to take ownership of the treasured heirloom, so they decided to donate it somewhere anyone could appreciate it. For every holiday, Beverly and Forrest's granddaughter Eudora stops by to decorate the dollhouse with different festive pieces her grandmother collected and created over the years. And even after spending so much time with it, she admits she notices something new with every visit.

The dollhouse may not be as hands-on as some of the other exhibits at the Portland Children's Museum, but it just might be its most special.

Address 4015 SW Canyon Road, Portland, OR 97221, +1 (503) 223-6500, www.portlandcm.org, info@portlandcm.org | Getting there MAX to Washington Park (Red & Blue Lines); TriMet to MAX/Oregon Zoo (Line 63); Washington Park Shuttle; metered on-site parking lot | Hours Daily 9am–5pm | Tip After the museum, take the kids to Finnegan's Toys & Gifts to peruse its vast selection of unique and rare toys, puzzles, and more (820 SW Washington Street, www.finneganstoys.com).

10_Blue Collar Wrestling
Pro wrestling high in drama, low in glitz

Every Sunday since 2010, the Fraternal Order of Eagles in North Portland transforms into the venue for Blue Collar Wrestling (BCW). A dozen or so men and women suit up each week to perform a scripted bill, but this isn't a glitzy production like you'd see on World Wrestling Entertainment. These wrestlers live in the DIY world. The costumes are modest – overalls, bedazzled jackets, occasional face paint – the props are cheap, but the drama is real. And so is the fan base.

By the time the bell rings at 6pm, the place is packed. One to two hundred spectators have paid their $10 admission and taken a seat around the ring placed in the middle of the Lodge. The particularly hardcore fans sit eagerly at ringside tables. Before the action begins, co-owner Pattie Deitz shuffles around the room, handing out the evening's itinerary while chatting with regulars. One wall is dedicated to merch tables, allowing fans to support their favorite characters outside the ring. Beer and liquor will cost you less than $5, as will concessions like hot dogs, nachos, and chili.

As the emcee begins his preamble to the night's events, the inner circle is chanting and cheering, right on cue. By the time the first match begins, those in the know have already picked sides, shouting support to their champion and "YOU SUCK!" to the opponent. Each bout comes with a backstory, as the wrestlers are divided into rivaling factions, like The Moonshiners, The Freak Show, and The Brandt Dynasty, and each clan comes with its own loyal fan base. The evening is generally divided into three matches, then intermission, followed by a Semi Main Event and Main Event that range from Tag Teams to Fall Count Anywhere matches.

By the time it's all over, regulars get emotional about the night's outcomes while first-timers leave their seats with a grin regardless, soaking in the spectacle they've just witnessed.

Address 7611 N Exeter Avenue, Portland, OR 97203, +1 (503) 757-3132, www.facebook.com/pg/bluecollarwrestlingpdx | **Getting there** TriMet to N Lombard & Clarendon (Line 75) or N Portsmouth & Lombard (Line 35); on-site parking lot | **Hours** Sun 6pm–close | **Tip** Grab a bite at Deitz' restaurant, Patties Home Plate Café, less than two miles from the Fraternal Order of Eagles (8501 N Lombard Street).

11___Bobbie the Wonder Dog
Here lies a very good boy

On a cold February day in 1924, Frank and Elizabeth Brazier opened the front door to find their dog Bobbie on the stoop. Normally, this wouldn't be a shocking sight; however, this particular Scotch collie mix had disappeared during a family road trip to Indiana – six months earlier.

Mangy, emaciated, and paws worn to the bone, the two-year-old dog braved the winter and trekked over 2,500 miles, including crossing the Continental Divide, to get back to his home in Silverton, Oregon. The local paper published a story about Bobbie's amazing journey, and the miraculous news quickly spread nationally. The Braziers received hundreds of letters addressed to "Silverton's Bobbie" and "Bobbie the Wonder Dog," with many claiming they had encountered him on the long walk home.

The celebrated collie received accolades, including medals and keys to cities. His story was featured in *Ripley's Believe It Or Not* and *Bobbie, A Great Collie*. The very good boy even became a movie star, playing himself in the silent film *The Call of the West*.

When Bobbie the Wonder Dog passed away in 1927, the Braziers requested he be laid to rest in the Oregon Humane Society (OHS) pet cemetery, where he was buried with honors. Portland's Mayor George Baker gave the eulogy at his funeral. A week later, German shepherd Hollywood star Rin Tin Tin draped a wreath across Bobbie's grave.

The public can still visit Bobbie today. Though over 2,000 pets have been laid to rest at OHS by their owners, Bobbie's grave is hard to miss. He resides in an eternal white doghouse trimmed in red that he was gifted at the Portland Home Show, with his name engraved on a plaque above the door. While you're visiting the legendary dog, think about taking home one of your own. OHS adopts out over 10,000 dogs, cats, and small animals per year and boasts a 98% save rate, making it the safest community in America for homeless pets.

BOBBIE
OF
SILVERTON

LOST AUG. 15, 1923 AT WOLCOTT IND.
RETURNED TO SILVERTON ORE. FEB. 15, 1924
DIED APRIL 6, 1927
OWNED BY MR. & MRS. GEO. BRAZIER

Address 1067 NE Columbia Boulevard, Portland, OR 97211, +1 (503) 285-7722, www.oregonhumane.org | **Getting there** Free on-site parking lot | **Hours** Sun–Wed 10am–7pm, Thu–Sat 10am–9pm | **Tip** Visit Bobbie's hometown of Silverton, and check out a mural dedicated to his life on the town's busiest street (200 S Water Street, Silverton, OR 97381).

12__Bonito's *Il Femminiello*
18th-century LGBTQ+ *painting at the PAM*

Like many metropolis art collections, the Portland Art Museum (PAM) houses some remarkable pieces by famous artists. Paintings by the likes of Pierre-Auguste Renoir, Vincent Van Gogh, Albert Bierstad, and Cecco di Pietro adorn the walls of the 112,000-square-foot gallery space. One of the museum's most prized possessions is Claude Monet's early 20th-century masterpiece *Le Bassin aux Nymphéas* (*The Waterlily Pond*). However, perhaps more than its impressive collection of famed works, PAM prides itself on representing the underrepresented.

In the Mary and Pete Mark Gallery of post-17th-century European art hangs *Il Femminiello*, a mid-18th-century oil painting by Italian artist Giuseppe Bonito. The recently discovered piece showcases Naples' acceptance of crossdressers, known as *femminielli*, which translates to "little female-men." The painting's subject is a *femminiello* being fitted for a coral necklace – both he and the jewelry were traditionally thought to bring good luck. Though Neapolitans embraced *femminielli*, this painting is the only known representation until the 19th century. The same gallery houses *Portrait of a Man Seated at a Desk*, a piece by Marianne Loir, an 18th-century, female, French artist working in a time and place where academies refused admittance to women. PAM also has an extensive Native American collection, housed in the Confederated Tribes of Grand Ronde Center for Native American Art. Notable for its diversity and depth, the collection comprises 5,000 prehistoric and historic pieces created by 200 different cultural groups throughout North America, including works by Maria Martinez, Allan Houser, and Lillian Pitt.

With a permanent collection composed of over 40,000 works of art, and breathtaking temporary exhibits, the museum provides the opportunity to discover something new and awe-inspiring each time you visit.

Address 1219 SW Park Avenue, Portland, OR 97205, +1 (503)226-2811,
www.portlandartmuseum.org, info@pam.org | Getting there TriMet to SW Jefferson &
10th (Lines 6, 38, 45, 55, 58, 68, 92, & 96); Portland Streetcar to Art Museum (A Loop &
NS Lines); metered street parking | Hours Tue & Wed 10am 5pm, Thu & Fri 10am–8pm,
Sat & Sun 10am–5pm | Tip Less than a mile away from the Portland Art Museum is
Gallery 114, a self-governing community of artists championing artistic freedom
(1100 NW Glisan Street, www.gallery114pdx.com).

13 ___ Boys Fort

A study in "manthropology"

Jake France and Richard Rolfe built a fort in downtown Portland with the mantra "Everyone deserves a fort, and this is it." Those curious enough to enter will discover treasures like slingshots, toys, pennants, books, vintage posters, and other necessities for anyone who's still young at heart.

When the friends started Boys Fort in 2011, it was with the idea that it'd be a holiday pop-up shop – a one-time thing. They rallied together a band of local makers and thoughtfully organized a collection of male-centric merchandise. But the holidays came and went, and the duo continued receiving calls about particular items. It took years for them to embrace fully their "manthropology" calling, but they gave in. Now they're running a specialty store that's both nostalgic and nothing like you've ever seen.

The fort currently represents anywhere between 50 and 60 local makers (over half of whom are female). Their bestseller is the Archie's Press collection – intricate maps of cities, human anatomy, zodiac signs, food and drink items, and more. The creator was Boys Fort's first artist and intern. At first, he only sold a map of Portland. Now he has over 400 unique prints. One of France's favorite pieces is the Cutting Board Project. Each board is made with scraps from other projects, and their tags tell you what kind of wood they're made out of and where the rest of the wood is – from dressers in Northwest Portland to the San Francisco Museum of Art. But no matter the item, France and Rolfe love all their suppliers equally.

"The best part is that once a month we get to write a check to someone we *really* like," Rolfe gushes. "We've become great friends with everyone we represent. That's my favorite part about the job."

While the store specializes in items for men, it's not exclusive to men only. "Don't let the name fool you," France assures. "Boys Fort's for everybody."

Address 1001 SW Morrison Street, Portland, OR 97205, +1 (503) 241-2855, www.boysfort.com | **Getting there** MAX Galleria & SW 10th (Blue & Red Lines); metered street parking | **Hours** Mon–Sat 11am–6pm, Sun 11am–5pm | **Tip** If you want to frame your newly purchased Archie Map, head around the corner to Mel's Frame Shop, a full-service custom frame store that repurposes scrap molding to make one-of-a-kind, affordable, pre-made frames (1007 SW Morrison Street, www.melsframeshop.com).

14___ The Candy Basket
Home of the 21-foot chocolate waterfall

On the city's outskirts resides Portland's own chocolate factory. It may not be run by an eccentric man in a velvet jacket and top hat, and no peculiar orange workers patrol the premises, but The Candy Basket is filled with its own magic.

As you enter, a 21-foot chocolate waterfall cascades before your eyes. A heating system keeps the chocolate melted, while an electrical pump sucks the gooey liquid through 50 feet of heavy-duty piping from the bronze-plated pool at the bottom to the marble top of the falls. Designed by the factory's owner Dale Fuhr, the fountain has been pumping 2,700 pounds of sweet goodness since the early 1990s and is the largest continuous chocolate waterfall in the world.

Fuhr grew up next door to Kipi Doran. Dale was the Chocolate King (his family bought The Candy Basket in 1970), and Kipi was the Taffy Queen (her family has owned Shorthill Taffy since 1960). In 1994, Kipi acquired Shorthill and called up her old friend Dale to talk business. Their professional relationship quickly turned romantic. Six months into their romance, though, Dale's father died. In 1999, the couple bought The Candy Basket from Dale's family and merged the two companies. Together, they've grown their own family business into one of the largest confectionery distributors in the Pacific Northwest.

Just below the waterfall, chocolate, taffy, and other sweets span as far as the eye can see in the factory retail store. For those who want to learn more about the process, tours are available several times a week. Visitors walk through the factory and watch as workers melt, mold, and dip chocolates, while others heat, pull, and flavor taffy – all using machinery that's over a century old. The Candy Basket is one of the last local chocolatiers to offer classic confections with old-fashioned creams and handmade treats. That love is palpable in all 120 chocolate and 180 taffy variations.

PLEASE
DO NOT
EAT OUR
CHOCOLATE CASCADE
WE GIVE
FREE SAMPLES

Address 1924 NE 181st Avenue, Portland, OR 97230, +1 (503) 666-2000, www.candybasketinc.com, online@candybasketinc.com | Getting there Free on-site parking lot | Hours Mon–Fri 9am–6pm, Sat 10am–5pm, Sun 11am–4pm; see website for tour information | Tip The husband-wife duo at Woodblock Chocolate make their own chocolate straight from the bean, with a café open daily for patrons to taste their treats in a variety of forms (1715 NE 17th Avenue, www.woodblockchocolate.com).

15__Cargo

Treasures from near and far

Before you even step inside Cargo, it's clear you're about to enter a world of whimsy. The foyer greets you with exotic plants snaking their way up from pots, while shimmering streamers and ornamental lanterns dangle from the ceiling. Upon entering you're hit with dazzling displays incorporating flowers, foliage, and breathtaking works of art that just so happen to be for sale.

Cargo is a 20,000-square-foot emporium that carries artisan goods from around the world. The business stemmed from owner Patty Merrill's love of travel. What began with bringing back whatever she could fit in her carry-on luggage has become a sprawling showroom filled with everything from Zodiac bobbleheads crafted by a Japanese family to patchwork quilts and hand-built furniture.

"Our philosophy is that retail is pretty predictable, and what brings us joy is the unpredictability," Merrill explains. "We want to show you things you've never seen before, or that you haven't seen in a long time."

Cargo also offers shared retail and maker spaces for local artists. "It's created a real community atmosphere," says co-owner Bridgid Blackburn. "In a time in Portland where rents are rising, it's been really great for us to figure out a way to carve out parts of the store to create a more sustainable model for everybody."

It's the people that really drive Cargo. Each item they sell tells a story, and they love collecting tales from customers too. Through thoughtful, vibrant displays and interesting products, Merrill and Blackburn have created an environment that encourages lingering. Families spend hours in the space; curious perusers bring their dogs and explore (just watch out for the shop cat, Calla Lily), and its owners wouldn't have it any other way.

"We don't have boring customers," Merrill says with a smile. "Everyone's in on the adventure."

Address 81 SE Yamhill Street, Portland, OR 97214, +1 (503) 209-8349, www.cargoinc.com, web@cargoinc.com | **Getting there** TriMet to Morrison Bridge (Line 15); free parking lot out back | **Hours** Daily 11am–6pm | **Tip** Stop by the in-store café Giraffe for mouthwatering Japanese deli fare to munch while exploring. Try the egg salad and pork katsu combo sandwich (81 SE Yamhill Street, www.giraffegoods.com).

16__ Carver Café
A dining destination for Twihards everywhere

The Carver Café is a small, unassuming diner right off OR-224 in the unincorporated community of Carver, Oregon. For years it was a place that locals frequented to dine on healthy doses of biscuits and gravy, burgers, and chowder. It was a locals-only kind of restaurant, where the server had your order cooking and a cup of coffee at your table practically before you even took a seat. But in 2008, that all changed.

Though set in Forks, Washington, the *Twilight* franchise scouted the Carver Café for its first film. As Twihards know, the restaurant is Bella's go-to place to grab a bite with her dad, Charlie Swan. (Fun fact: the series' author Stephenie Meyer makes a cameo sitting at the counter in the second scene. She orders a veggie plate.)

When the movie premiered, people from all over the globe flocked to Carver to see where the Swans liked to eat. For a year straight, the café was jam-packed with fans eager for a photo op and chance to sign the guestbook. Some traveled from as far as Japan, Australia, Europe, and South America to take a seat at the famous corner table preferred by Bella and Charlie.

Today the Carver Café still gets the occasional fan dropping by, but the staff knows to prepare itself in the month of September, when Twihards like to celebrate Bella's birthday (September 13) at the restaurant. For those who aren't aware of the diner's association with the *Twilight* franchise, fear not. The Carver isn't decked out in movie memorabilia, aside from a handful of dolls sitting on a shelf. However, there are a few hidden pieces of the film that still live within the café's walls. Archival black-and-white photos of Forks hang on the wood-paneled walls, as do a set of antlers.

And though you may not be able to order a spinach salad or garden burger like Bella, the Carver Café serves hearty portions of delicious and comforting American favorites.

Address 16471 OR-224, Damascus, OR 97089, +1 (503) 658-3206 | **Getting there** Free parking in on-site lot | **Hours** Mon–Fri 6:30am–2pm, Sat & Sun 8am–2pm | **Tip** In Portland, on the edge of Forest Park, sits the extravagant modern house in which the Cullen family resided in the *Twilight* movies (3333 NW Quimby Street).

17 Casa Diablo

"We put the meat on the pole, not on the plate"

On September 19, 2006, Johnny Diablo Žūklė opened Pirate's Tavern in industrial Northwest Portland. That date just so happens to be National Talk Like a Pirate Day, but this restaurant was so much more than a swashbuckling eatery, it was Žūklė's way of introducing a new vegan joint to the city. Unfortunately, the blue collar patrons that walked through his doors every day were not fond of animal-free eats. A year after opening, the vegan restaurateur found his back against the wall as he stared down potential bankruptcy.

"I thought to get the mostly male workers in the area to come in and give the food a try I had to have some sort of attraction, any kind of gimmick. I thought to myself, *could beautiful women be the answer to attracting men to vegan cuisine and hopefully open their hearts to a more compassionate way of living?*" Žūklė recalls. "If I failed I may taint the true mission of veganism: to save animals from cruelty and death. So I reached out to the animal spirits and asked them what they wanted me to do. After a long time I received my answer. 'We are dying! Save us,' I heard. 'Do whatever it takes.' So I said, 'Yes. I will.'"

In February 2008, Žūklė opened Casa Diablo: the world's first vegan strip club. "Vixens not veal. Sizzle not steak. We put the meat on the pole, not on the plate," is the venue's motto, and the dimly lit club lives up to it. Dancers aren't allowed to wear fur, leather, wool, silk, or feathers onstage, and diners can choose from an extensive vegan food menu that includes everything from the Diablo burger and fries (Žūklė's favorite) to beefy stroganoff made with soy strips.

As Casa Diablo's success builds, Žūklė hopes others follow in his footsteps.

"It's a win-win-win situation for everyone," he explains, "for humans' health, the planet's environment, and most of all for the love and compassion of all living creatures."

Address 2839 NW St. Helens Road, Portland, OR 97210, +1 (503) 222-6600, www.facebook.com/CasaDiablo | Getting there Free parking in on-site lot | Hours Daily 2pm–2:30am | Tip Casa Diablo has been so successful that Žūklė opened a second location, Dusk Til' Dawn Casa Diablo 2 (8445 SE McLoughlin Boulevard).

18 Cathedral Park

Where young Thelma Taylor spent her last day alive

During the day, Cathedral Park is a beautiful place to spend an afternoon. Families pack picnics to enjoy on the bank of the Willamette River. Couples take romantic strolls to marvel at the towering St. Johns bridge above, its gothic stone pillars rising from the water. But when the sun sets and darkness falls, the park has a different feeling. An ominous feeling. Those who have visited at night swear they hear a girl calling for help. But who is she?

In the summer of 1949, Thelma Taylor was planning to pick beans in Hillsboro, but she never made it to her destination. While she was walking to the bus stop in the early morning of August 5, 22-year-old ex-convict Morris Leland lured the teenager into his stolen car. He took her to the riverbank, where he held her overnight. The brave girl vehemently denied his sexual advances, and when the sun began to rise Thelma's first instinct was to scream. Her captor hit her over the head repeatedly with a steel bar to quiet her, and then made sure she'd never speak again by stabbing her in the chest and side. Morris buried Thelma in a shallow grave under a pile of driftwood. She was only 15 years old.

Six days later, Morris was arrested for auto theft and confessed to Thelma's kidnapping and murder. During his trial, the troubled man pleaded not guilty by reason of insanity, but he was found guilty and sentenced to death on February 7, 1951. His sentence was carried out in January 1953 by way of lethal gas.

Though Thelma's life was taken eight blocks away from Cathedral Park, she is said to haunt the area to this day. Police have been called on numerous occasions in response to calls from visitors, who report hearing a girl crying, "Help! Somebody help me, please!" But each time authorities arrive, they're unable to locate the source of the screams. The paranormal events happen under the bridge, and always on summer nights.

Address N Edison Street and Pittsburg Avenue, Portland, OR 97203, +1 (503) 823-7529, www.portlandoregon.gov/parks | Getting there Street parking | Hours Daily 5am – midnight | Tip After exploring the park, take a walk across the St. Johns bridge and soak in spectacular views of the river and mountains (8600 NW Bridge Avenue).

19___Clary Sage Herbarium
A delicate balance between medicine and magic

Laurie Lava-Books has been fascinated by herbalism and magic her whole adult life. Though her heritage is Yurok/Karuk/Chimariko/Sasquatch/Northern European mix, her indigenous family was colonized, hindering her from a traditional Native American upbringing. In her early 20s, she took matters into her own hands and began digging deep into her ancestry. Lava-Books credits her bloodline for an innate curiosity with herbal medicine, and after years of studying and creating products of her own, she decided to open her own apothecary with nothing more than $1,000 in her pocket.

That was in 2011. Now, Clary Sage Herbarium resides on NE Alberta, attracting customers with its grounding energy. As soon as you walk in, your nostrils are filled with the soothing scent of herbs, tea, and incense. Though fragrant, the smell is not overwhelming. Nor is it synthetic. Lava-Books takes pride in her thoughtfully curated array of aromatherapy, herbal, body care, CBD, and ceremonial products.

"We make sure the companies we work with have integrity and are doing things the right way, sustainably," she says. "We irritate a lot of people by asking hard questions about their sourcing."

Clary Sage also carries Lava-Books' own natural medicine line, Two Spirit. The name is not only a nod to her indigenous heritage, but also her sexuality. The term is an all-inclusive phrase for Native members of the LGBTQ+ community. As for her products, she marries herbal extracts and flower essences with a bit of honey to create tinctures that aid in everything from anxiety to sexual and domestic trauma.

Aside from carrying quality products, Clary Sage is all about community and inclusivity. "We're a magic shop, but I want to make sure everybody feels welcome here," Lava-Books says. "If people come in here and they don't feel joy in their hearts, they're just dead to the world!"

Address 2901 NE Alberta Street, Portland, OR 97211, +1 (503) 236-6737, www.clarysageherbarium.com | Getting there TriMet to NE 30th & Alberta (Line 72); free street parking | Hours Daily 10am–6pm | Tip For those looking for a more clinical approach to herbs, head down the street to Vital Ways Holistic Clinical Herbalism (2714 NE Alberta Street, www.portlandherbalschool.com).

20 Cleary Sculpture Garden
Commemorating local literary royalty

Beverly Cleary is revered for her ability to write emotional realism, and most of her characters, including the pesky Ramona Quimby, are children from middle-class families. Her stories are relatable because she writes about the minutiae of everyday life in a fascinating way, and her material comes from real-life experiences. The famed children's author grew up in Portland's Hollywood neighborhood. She used this setting and childhood memories in her novels. Cleary's fictional characters live on the very real Klickitat Street, named after the local Native American tribe (Cleary has said the name reminds her of the sound of knitting needles). Cleary's childhood home is on the neighboring Hancock Street.

Throughout her career, the beloved author wrote dozens of books that not only stole the hearts of children (and adults) worldwide, but also garnered prestigious awards. In 1981, she won the National Book Award for *Ramona and Her Mother*; three years later she was awarded the Newbery Medal for *Dear Mr. Henshaw*. Cleary has also received the National Medal of Arts, the Laura Ingalls Wilder Medal from the Association for Library Service to Children, and recognition as a Library of Congress Living Legend.

In 1995, Cleary's hometown commemorated her with a sculpture garden on the west end of Grant's Park, where she played as a child. Local artist Lee Hunt erected three bronze statues depicting Cleary's most iconic characters: Ramona Quimby, Henry Huggins, and his dog Ribsy, built around a splash fountain. When the water is turned on, it looks like they're splashing in puddles (one of Ramona's favorite pastimes). Granite plaques surround the statues, engraved with the titles of Cleary's books.

Right down the street is the Beverly Cleary School, a public school that serves K-8 and funnels into Grant High School, where its namesake graduated in the 1930s.

Address Grant Park Path near NE 33rd & Brazee, Portland, OR 97212, +1 (503) 823-7529, www.portlandoregon.gov/parks | Getting there TriMet to NE 33rd & Brazee (Line 70); free street parking | Hours Daily 5am–midnight | Tip Walk a few blocks south and check out the 1910 bungalow that was Cleary's childhood home (3340 NE Hancock Street).

21__Crystal Ballroom

Explore the history of the "floating" ballroom

Most Portlanders know McMenamins' Crystal Ballroom is a great place to see live music. But you didn't know the property offers free daily tours for visitors to learn a little more about the famous 'floating' ballroom, did you?

Guests congregate at Ringlers Pub, located on the Crystal's floor level, where a guide greets them at 2pm. Before ascending the staircase (or elevator for those who request it), the tour guide gives a brief history of the ballroom's origins. A man named Montrose Ringler opened the venue, originally called Cotillion Hall, in 1914 as a place for people to gather for good times drinking and dancing. Look for the original wooden sign that is hanging in Ringlers Pub near the pinball machines.

From there, the tour goes up to an on-site brewery before entering Lola's Room, where you'll hear what's probably the most interesting story of the day. The bar is named after Lola Baldwin, America's first female police officer and Portland's Disciplinary Officer. During the Prohibition Era, Portland also implemented a dancing prohibition that banned partners from getting too close on the dance floor. Since Cotillion Hall violated both laws, Ringler and Baldwin butted heads, and she made it her life's work to shut him down. After years of slapping fines on him with the threat of jail time, she eventually ran him out of town and subsequently retired. When the McMenamin brothers purchased the property in 1997, they ironically named a bar dedicated to dance parties and booze – the two things Baldwin hated – to the historic cop. Her portrait is also painted on a boiler that can be viewed from the Lola's Room landing.

The last stop is the ballroom itself. Here, you'll learn how the Cotillion transformed into the Crystal and where that legendary bouncy flooring gets its spring – all while sipping one of McMenamins' libations, if you so please.

Address 1332 W Burnside Street, Portland, OR 97209, +1 (503) 225-0047, www.crystalballroompdx.com | **Getting there** TriMet to West Burnside & SW 13th (Line 20); metered street parking | **Hours** Tours daily at 2pm, call for reservation | **Tip** Get your record shopping fix across the street at Everyday Music (1313 West Burnside Street, www.everydaymusic.com).

22   Darcelle XV

The oldest performing drag queen in the world

A night at the Darcelle XV Showplace is unlike any other. You'll laugh. You'll cry. You'll see an 89-year-old drag queen sing "Rhinestone Cowboy" in bedazzled, assless chaps.

"We've always tried to do this: when you walk in the door, leave everything out there. Smile, laugh, have fun, but take care of your problems somewhere else," says Walter Cole, aka Darcelle XV. "We also don't take our problems onstage."

That sentiment, and the love and support from Portland for over 50 years, is what keeps the female impersonator performing six times a week, even in the midst of tragedy. "My partner of 47 years [Roxy Neuhardt] died on Saturday evening at 5:15pm, and I was on stage at 8 o'clock," Cole recalls about his lover's passing in 2017. "I had to, for him and for me."

While Darcelle emcees each night, cracking jokes and singing songs, she's accompanied by an ensemble of beauties who put on a dazzling Las Vegas-style cabaret show filled with lip-syncing and dancing to timeless hits but aren't afraid to express who they really are in hilariously revealing ways. Since opening its doors in 1967 as the Demas Tavern, the Showplace has become a City of Roses institution, and Darcelle an icon. In 2016, Cole was recognized by the *Guinness World Records* as the oldest performing drag queen, and he shows no signs of slowing down.

"I know I'm not going to retire... but I'll do it until I can't. In 50+ years I have never said 'I don't want to go to work tonight.'" And he wants his fans to live with that same mindset. "If you're not happy, find something else to do," he declares. "Find your place. Find who you are."

Cole's love of Darcelle is palpable at every show, and it's the audience that feeds it. "When I can look out and I see a smile," Cole says, "that's why we do it... We touch people sometimes without even knowing. It's rewarding. It's wonderful."

Address 3522 N Vancouver Avenue, Portland, OR 97227, +1 (503) 477-6090, www.diybar.co, portland@diybar.co | Getting there TriMet to N Vancouver & Beech (Linc 44) or N Vancouver & Fremont (Line 4); free street parking | Hours Tue–Fri 3–10pm, Sat 11am–10pm, Sun 11am–6pm | Tip Though DIY BAR doesn't serve food, there's a great 'locavore-oriented' sandwich shop called Brass Tacks right across the street (3535 N Vancouver Avenue, www.brasstackssandwiches.com).

24___Dockside Saloon Dumpster
The site of Tonya Harding's downfall

On January 30, 1994 Kathy Peterson was doing what she did most Sundays: catching up on cleaning and maintenance at her restaurant, the Dockside Saloon. While taking out the trash, she noticed the dumpster was filled with someone else's garbage. Frustrated, she went through it in hopes of finding a name and contacting the culprit.

Peterson found a check stub from the US Figure Skating Association addressed to Tonya Harding; she found a commuter ticket out of Detroit; she found papers with Jeff Gillooly's name on them; she found an envelope with handwritten information regarding Nancy Kerrigan's practice schedule at Tony Kent Arena. The writing would later be determined as Harding's.

Astonished by her discovery, Peterson called the FBI and stuffed any pertinent findings into her car trunk. In the weeks that followed, "all hell broke loose." Reporters from around the world visited Dockside for interviews; the phone rang off the hook. She testified before a grand jury and US Figure Skating Association panel. It was a lot.

"When it finally starts to sink in that while I'm not responsible, because people make their own decisions, I had a huge part in taking her down," Peterson recalls. "It was really stressful. I lost 10 pounds."

Though she played an important role in Harding's downfall, Peterson never once considered marketing her restaurant as a tourist trap. "We didn't capitalize on it, because I didn't feel right about that," she says. "She's led a hard life."

The only Harding references you'll see at Dockside are a small portrait above the bar and the infamous dumpster story on the back of the menu. In fact, the skater has never even visited the restaurant, causing Peterson to question why the evidence was dumped there.

"Someday, maybe our paths will cross in a real way and we can have a conversation," she says. "Until then, it's just all for conjecture."

Address 2047 NW Front Avenue, Portland, OR 97209, +1 (503) 241-6433, www.docksidesaloon.com, dockside@docksidesaloon.com | **Getting there** TriMet to NW Front & 17th (Line 16); free street parking | **Hours** Mon–Fri 6am–9pm, Sat 6am–4pm, Sun 7am–3pm | **Tip** Skate on the same ice as Tonya Harding at the Lloyd Center Ice Rink (953 Lloyd Center, www.lloydice.com). Harding began skating there at the age of 4.

25__Eastside Distilling

Spirits by one of the US' first women distillers

In the 1970s, the Willamette Valley put Oregon on the map as a premiere wine making region. A decade later, Portland began leading the charge in the craft beer movement. Now, the city's making its presence known in the craft spirit scene. And Eastside Distilling is one of the first to open up shop in what's now called Distillery Row. Founded in 2008, the company began as a rum importer and has since become a purveyor of nearly 20 spirits. Their offerings include the famous Burnside Whiskey portfolio; a variety of potato vodka flavors, including marionberry and habanero; spiced and coffee flavored rum; gin; and tequila.

Guests who visit Eastside's tasting room can choose from a flight menu that has a little something for everyone. Whiskey lover? Choose a handful of the distillery's own award-winning whiskeys to try. Want to taste a variety of liquors? Create your own flight from Eastside's diverse list of spirits. Curious about the distillery's top-selling products? Taste their most popular spirits: Portland Potato Vodka, Hue-Hue Coffee Rum, Marionberry Whiskey, Burnside Oregon Oaked Bourbon, and Big Bottom Ninety-One Gin.

The company is a pioneer, and so is Mel Heim, Eastside Distillery's master distiller/blender and executive vice president of operations. After working as an assistant distiller for Rogue Ale & Spirits, the alcohol enthusiast took a job with Eastside in 2012 and became one of the American craft spirits scene's first female distillers. Under her leadership, the distillery's popular spirits have won over 40 medals for flavor. Heim believes in collaboration over competition, mentoring other women in the industry, and serving as a Women of Vine and Spirits committee member.

Though Eastside's original location is the one on Distillery Row, they also have retail locations in Northwest Portland and in the Washington Square and Clackamas malls.

Address 1512 SE 7th Avenue, Portland, OR 97214, +1 (971) 703-4712,
www.eastsidedistilling.com, info@eastsidedistilling.com| **Getting there** TriMet to SE 7th
& Clay (Line 2); metered street parking| **Hours** Mon–Fri 1–7pm, Sat & Sun 1–8pm |
Tip Interested in checking out the other distilleries in Distillery Row? Visit the collective's
website to learn more about passports and tour packages (www.distilleryrowpdx.com).

26 __ Echo Chamber
Pioneer Courthouse Square's happy accident

Pioneer Courthouse Square was a school, a hotel, and a parking garage before becoming the open-air plaza that it is today. In fact, the block itself dates back to 1856.

In the 1970s, Portland's Downtown Plan proposed open space development of the square block and launched an international design competition before landing on Will Martin's idea. When construction began, funding became a problem, but then the project was saved by $750,000 raised through the sale of 50,000 bricks inscribed with donors' names. Those bricks now make up the surface of "Portland's Living Room." However, there's another aspect of the square that may not have been in the original design plans.

On the west end of Pioneer Courthouse Square sits the Small Amphitheater, designed as a pint-sized alternative for public events and with the purpose of adding humor without compromising the plaza's dignity and elegance. A half-circle of tier bricks surrounds the miniature meeting place, creating a seating area for spectators, while another circular pattern at the base directs the eye to one round brick in the middle. If you stand on that special brick and direct your voice toward the amphitheater seating area, something bizarre happens: your voice amplifies and bounces back at you.

You're standing in a tiny echo chamber.

The phenomenon occurs because sound waves ricochet off the slanted bricks and direct themselves back towards the speaker. But it only happens when you stand on that one particular brick, and the echoes are not heard by anyone outside the tiny chamber.

Though it seems like the echo chamber was strategically planned due to the brick design and the nature of a small-scale amphitheater, there are no signs of it in Martin's blueprint, nor is it indicated anywhere in the square. Could it be a happy accident? Go scope it out and see for yourself. Just don't talk about anything too personal.

Address 701 SW 6th Avenue, Portland, OR 97205, +1 (503) 223-1613, www.thesquarepdx.org |
Getting there MAX to Pioneer Square North (Blue & Red Lines); TriMet to SW 5th &
Morrison (Lines 1, 8, 12, 94, & Downtown Express); metered street parking | Hours Daily
5am–midnight | Tip Get a history lesson by visiting the neighboring Pioneer Courthouse,
which just happens to be the second-oldest federal courthouse in the West (700 SW
6th Avenue, www.pioneercourthouse.com).

27 ___ Elk Rock Garden
A secret garden in the heart of Dunthorpe

While driving along SW Military Lane, it's easy to think you've gotten the directions wrong. *This can't be right,* you think as you slowly pass extravagant house after extravagant house. *I'm in a residential neighborhood.* But when you get to the end of the road, you've reached your destination. Though it seems like a peculiar location, Elk Rock Garden was once a private residence itself.

When Scotland native Peter Kerr built his grand estate in 1914, he picked a spectacular location. Elk Rock Bluff, in what is now the Dunthorpe neighborhood, towers over the Willamette River and boasts views of Mount Hood to the east. The 13-acre property was prime for Kerr to build his Scottish manse and dabble in his real passion: gardening.

In 1916, the Scotsman began work on his extensive, English-style garden. He paved winding paths throughout the estate that lead to fish ponds, meditative terraces and unobstructed views of the breathtaking river below. He planted hundreds of botanical treasures, from rare magnolias and chrysanthemums to witch hazel and soaring oak trees. Kerr dutifully maintained his garden for nearly six decades, until he passed away in 1957 at the age of 95.

Upon his death, the businessman's daughters Anne McDonald and Jane Platt gifted the estate, along with an endowment for maintenance, to the Episcopal Bishop of Oregon under the stipulation that it be open to the public.

Today, Elk Rock Garden at the Bishop's Close is thriving. Kerr's magnificent manor is now the Episcopal Diocese of Oregon's offices. The grounds are open and free to the public daily, allowing visitors to wind down in their favorite tranquil nook or discover a new part of the garden whenever they please. And though equally expansive as the famous Japanese Gardens, this lush neighborhood oasis is still a well-kept secret, making it a nice reprieve from tourist crowds.

Address 11800 SW Military Lane, Portland, OR 97219, +1 (503) 636-5613, www.elkrockgarden.org | Getting there TriMet to SW Riverside & Military (Lines 35 & 36); free on-site parking lot | Hours Daily 8am–5pm | Tip The Grotto is another spectacular botanical garden with religious affiliations. The Catholic sanctuary emits a peaceful energy, and its winter holiday festivities can't be beat (8840 NE Skidmore Street, www.thegrotto.org).

28 Fido's

A doggone good time

Scott Porter is a businessman. After spending years as an Air Force pilot, the entrepreneur had a hand in numerous endeavors, from sales and marketing ventures to delivery services. When a new taproom opened up in Beaverton, he thought he had his next business opportunity. But after visiting six competing establishments, they all started to blend together. He scrapped the idea. Then a trip to a cat café changed everything.

When Porter and his son stepped into the café, they were bombarded with a long list of rules that all began with "No." They couldn't approach the felines, and the skittish kitties wouldn't come near them. "This would be a lot different with dogs," his son quipped. And that's when the lightbulb turned on.

Three years and countless hours of research later, Porter opened Fido's, billed as the World's First Dog Tap House. Tucked away in a Walmart parking lot in the Portland suburb of Tigard, the pub offers a rotating list of 40 beers, ciders, and wine on tap; an extensive food menu boasting everything from personal pizzas to kimchi chicken rice bowls; and, most importantly, adoptable dogs.

As soon as you step through the door, Porter is there to greet you with a smile, unless he's tending to the pups. The beer menu illuminates straight ahead, underneath a sign that reads, *Eat. Drink. Adopt!* To the right is a large windowed room where three to six doggos can be seen roaming around, taking a nap, or playing with other patrons. The friendly little canines come from Oregon Friends of Shelter Animals, a nonprofit with a mission to save homeless pets from high-kill shelters.

For a four-dollar "donation," visitors can play in the dog room for 30 minutes and even take a four-legged friend home with them after completing the adoption process, of course. The beer is good, but Porter doesn't allow for drunk impulse buys here.

Address 7700 SW Dartmouth Street, Suite 110, Tigard, OR 97223, +1 (503) 941-5757, www.ilovefidos.com, ilovefidos@gmail.com | **Getting there** Free parking in lot | **Hours** Tue 3–9pm, Wed & Thu 3–10pm, Fri & Sat 11:30am–10pm, Sun 11:30am–9pm | **Tip** For more doggone good times, visit the Hip Hound in Northwest Portland. The pet boutique offers an array of holistic foods, as well as toys and apparel for your fur babies (610 NW 23rd Avenue, www.hiphoundshop.com).

29__Fly Awake Tea House
A place for tea aficionados and delightful weirdos

Tucked away in an alley off bustling Mississippi is a nondescript door with a handwritten sign that says, *Fly Awake Tea House*. It's hard to find if you're not looking for it, which was not coincidental.

Inside, murals cover the walls as shop owner Kevin von Behren brews teas in the Chinese style of *Gongfu*. It translates to "making tea with skill," but this tea maker interprets it as "being present." Using a small clay teapot called a *gaiwan*, he meticulously brews Chinese oolongs, *pu-erh* cakes, white teas, or whatever is in season, striving to give customers the best experience he can.

"I have a pretty strong hypothesis that this kind of attention and this kind of care transfers to how it feels when you actually drink it," he proclaims while steeping a cup of Golden Water Turtle oolong behind the wooden bar. "I want to make sure every single person gets that experience."

This is why he keeps Fly Awake hidden and small: he's devoted to interacting with his patrons as much as possible. This is also why he connected with *Gongfu* style, which he compares to a pub. Like a bartender, the person serving tea is the one paying attention while everyone else interacts.

Although the tea is important – von Behren only sources leaves from specific Chinese farms – it's not the first reason why Fly Awake exists. To its owner, the communal aspect is what makes his tea house so special. He wanted to create a safe space for people to meet and talk comfortably. To him, success is seeing customers form genuine relationships – the tea is just a vehicle for that connection.

"The people who hang out here are the most delightful weirdos I've ever met," von Behren gushes. "It really attracts a very interesting style of person."

Even if you don't meet your soulmate at Fly Awake, there's a very good chance you'll have a one-of-a-kind tea-drinking experience.

Address 909 N Beech Street, Suite B, Portland, OR 97227, +1 (503) 867-8905, www.flyawakepdx.com | **Getting there** TriMet to N Mississippi & Beech (Line 4); free street parking | **Hours** Daily noon–8pm | **Tip** If you prefer your tea leaves mixed with other goodies, head over to Brew Dr. Tea Company right down the street for a wide selection of loose-leaf tea (3917 N Mississippi Avenue, www.brewdrtea.com).

30__Freakybuttrue Peculiarium

Don't believe everything that you see

The Freakybuttrue Peculiarium is known for its "Keep Portland Weird" ethos and Instagram-worthy photo ops (where else can you take a picture on Krampus' lap or snap a shot of your friend getting flayed by aliens?). But what a lot of visitors skim past is the gallery's hilarious wit and drive to keep skepticism alive.

"Our 'truthiness' is a response to all the spin and fake news, to remind people to stay on their toes and don't trust anything because it looks 'true'," explains founder Mike Wellins. "And this idea works well because people often blow through the gallery and take things at face value."

The first piece of deliberate deception is thrown at you before ever stepping foot inside the peculiarium. The signage above the front door reads *Established 1972*, which is far from the truth. Wellins and his partner Lisa Freeman opened Freakybuttrue in April 2011 as a space to celebrate their love of sci-fi, urban legend, and all things strange. A massive Sasquatch greets you upon entering; a haunted dollhouse depicting gruesome murder scenes is on display; an interactive video installation allows you to step inside a zombie brain. Though these exhibits are clearly make-believe, there are others, like the remnants of spontaneous human combustion and detailed account of the victim, that could be believable – if you don't read closely enough.

"For those who read and look close, there's many levels of lampooning, teasing and nonsense," Wellins says before recalling a pair of guests who read every bit of signage in the gallery, giggling along the way. "They feel like they're in on a secret, and they are. That's very satisfying for me to hear." That being said, not *everything* in the gallery is fake. You just have to decipher fact from fiction.

A small entrance fee gets you into the peculiarium, which is waived for those visiting in costume and any four-legged companions.

Address 640 SE Stark Street, Portland, OR 97214, +1 (503) 227-3164, www.peculiarium.com, peculiarium@freakybuttrue.com | **Getting there** TriMet to SE Grand & Stark (Line 6); free street parking | **Hours** Mon, Wed–Sat 10am–7pm | **Tip** Assuming you don't lose your appetite after visiting the Peculiarium, grab a bite to eat at Le Bistro Montage, under the Morrison Bridge. We suggest the Spold Mac (301 SE Morrison Street, www.montageportland.com).

31 Fumerie Parfumerie
Shop for luxe fragrances in a welcoming atmosphere

Stepping inside Fumerie Parfumerie is like stepping into a different era. An early 20th-century soundtrack plays ballads and jazz; spherical Edison lightbulbs hang over the wooden bar; ornate Persian rugs blanket the floor; exposed brick frames the shop's front corners. And the smell. Oh, the smell. Proprietress Tracy Tsefalas likens it to the alluring scent of baked goods wafting from a bakery into the air, only she's enticing patrons with the intoxicating scent of luxe fragrances.

Tsefalas has been educating the Richmond neighborhood on high-end fragrances since 2016, but her experience in the business began long before. Years ago, she married into a family that ran a fragrance boutique. Though the marriage didn't work out, she continued managing the store, and her passion grew, especially when it came to small, independent lines – she loved their sense of creativity. When it was time to move on from the family business and start her own, Tsefalas made it a point to specialize in innovative perfumers – you won't find any mass-marketed fragrance lines here. But perhaps even more important to her is building a sense of community.

Tsefalas will be the first to admit the world of fragrance can be intimidating, and her goal is to break down those barriers with a relaxing, welcoming atmosphere. The shop is designed for one-on-one interaction, with the bar its focal point. Patrons are encouraged to consult with a staff member about their preferences in hopes of finding the scent that best suites them. In addition to taking a personal approach with customers, Fumerie also hosts monthly events that range from fragrance swaps to presentations given by featured perfumers.

"I want people who come into my store to feel comfortable and have an experience," Tsefalas says. "Just settle in. As much as you want to learn, I'll take you there."

Address 3584 SE Division Street, Portland, OR 97202, +1 (234) 386-3743, www.fumerie.com, info@fumerie.com | Getting there TriMet to SE Division & 36th (Line 2); free street parking | Hours Tue–Sat 11am–7pm, Sun noon–4pm | Tip Right across the street from Fumerie Parfumerie, you'll find donna and toots – a women's clothing boutique that also specializes in fabrics and offers sewing classes (3574 SE Division Street, www.donnaandtoots.com).

32 _ Funhouse Lounge
Enter the Clown Room – if you dare

Funhouse Lounge describes itself as "theater without the safety net," and you'd be hard pressed to think of a more spot-on catchphrase for this venue, which is weird even by Portland standards. Thought of as a modern cabaret, Funhouse offers a wide variety of entertainment from stand-up comedy and improv, to karaoke and burlesque, to plays and bingo, and because anything goes, none of these shows are conventional. Regularly occurring programming includes SMUT (a somewhat X-rated stand-up comedy and burlesque showcase), Comic Strip (stand-up comedy where the comics strip during their sets), Rusty Trombone Bingo (this one actually isn't as dirty as it sounds), and DOMPROV (improv overseen by a dominatrix).

Though the 90-person theater is the venue's focal point, Funhouse is also a great place to grab a drink and some grub whether or not you're catching a show. The bar offers reasonably priced beer, wine, and liquor, and greasy pub food to go with it. The seating may not be abundant in this part of the venue, but that's okay – you'll probably be too busy admiring the décor to sit down anyway. The front part of the bar is decorated like your grandma's living room (if your grandma loved pop culture), adorned with couches and a fireplace. Portraits of Elvis Presley, Bruce Lee, Frida Kahlo, Gilda Radner, and more famous faces hang above the mantel.

But it's the Clown Room that guests seek out upon their first visit to Funhouse. Tucked away (so as not to scare unsuspecting patrons), this dimly lit room is covered in clown paintings. There's portraits of sad hobo clowns, happy-go-lucky clowns, expertly detailed clowns, crudely painted clowns – there's even a clown replica of *The Last Supper*. It's equal parts intriguing and downright terrifying, but it's something you have to see (unless you suffer from coulrophobia, then definitely *don't* enter the Clown Room).

Address 2432 SE 11th Avenue, Portland, OR 97214, +1 (503) 841-6734, www.funhouselounge.com, info@funhouselounge.com | **Getting there** TriMet to SE 11th & Division (Line 70); free street parking | **Hours** Wed, Thu & Sat 6pm–midnight, Fri 6pm–2am, Sun 5–10pm; see website for show schedule | **Tip** If you like the utterly bizarre and/or have an affinity for clowns, grab a drink at nearby Creepy's (627 SE Morrison Street, www.creepys.business.site).

33 Gorge Model Railroad Club

One of the largest model railroad clubs in America

The Columbia Model Railroad Club (CMRC) has been giving train enthusiasts a place to meet and work on their hobby since 1947; however, it was in 1983 that the organization became one of the largest in the country. After moving locations for the second time, the club settled into its current home and began constructing an expansive layout.

The 60'×70' room is truly remarkable. Every inch of space is used to recreate the Columbia River Gorge in miniature form, with a blue carpeted aisle running down the middle to represent the river. Three miles of snaking track split into separate divisions: the dual track mainline, the Oregon Trunk Line, and the logging division.

Senior club members are required to spend 50 hours a year working on the scenery, and the attention to detail is impressive. The layout models the 1950s and is historically accurate, with over 300 vintage vehicles cruising the streets and a functional drive-in movie theater that plays films from the era. Iconic Oregon landmarks like Crown Point, Multnomah Falls and its lodge, as well as Portland's Union Station, Broadway and Steel Bridges, and Jackson Tower, are all exact replicas. More than 600 miniature people call the layout home.

Though CMRC prides itself in historical accuracy, members also like to have fun. Pay close attention, and you'll see a zebra playing baseball, a dinosaur parading with elephants, a UFO, a Dr. Who TARDIS, and even the Starship Enterprise and Klingon Battle Cruiser soaring above the city.

At any given time, the club consists of 120 or more members, with many logging 30-plus years of membership. Anyone who's interested in joining CMRC is encouraged to stop by on a Tuesday, or during the month of November, when the club runs its annual fundraising show.

Address 2505 N Vancouver Avenue, Portland, OR 97227, +1 (503) 288-7246, www.columbiagorgemodelrailroadclub.com, info@columbiagorgemodelrailroadclub.com | Getting there TriMet to N Vancouver & Page (Lines 4 & 44); small on-site parking lot | Hours Weekly meetings Tue 7:30pm; see website for train show and open-house schedule | Tip Train enthusiasts can also get their kicks at the Oregon Rail Heritage Center (2250 SE Water Avenue, www.orhf.org).

34_ Green Hop
Racially diversifying the cannabis industry

When Green Hop opened its doors in 2017, it was the first historical hip-hop dispensary in the world – but it's so much more than that. It's the first black-owned dispensary in Oregon, and its founders are using their platform to help racially diversify the industry.

At the time Nicole Kennedy and Karanja Crews set out to open a dispensary, they wanted to pay homage to the culture that helped normalize marijuana use. But as they began learning more about the industry, they quickly realized it was whitewashed. They heard horror stories from Black people with budtending licenses who couldn't get jobs, and when they did eventually find employment, they were accused of stealing, or their employers harassed and treated them disrespectfully.

During Green Hop's first year in business, the city awarded Kennedy and Crews a $96,000 grant for an apprenticeship program called the Green Hop Academy, which helps Black entrepreneurs get their foot in the door as budtenders and explore other parts of the industry from growing to processing.

"Right now we're focusing on bringing more people that look like us into the industry, because it's still hard for people to get a job," Kennedy explains.

Kennedy and Crews are also selective about the brands their store carries. They're conscious about the people they do business with and look into where they're putting their money before agreeing to put their products on Green Hop's shelves. Both growing up in the Vernon neighborhood where the dispensary is located, they also follow the "reintrification" mindset.

"They're gentrifying around you, but you come back to the neighborhood and be a pillar and representation and model. So instead of making your money and leaving, stay and reinvest in the community. That's what we're about," Kennedy says about reintrification. "When you shop here, you're supporting a bigger story."

Address 5515 NE 16th Avenue, Portland, OR 97211, +1 (971) 301-5859,
www.gogreenhop.com, info@gogreenhop.com | Getting there TriMet to NE 15th &
Killingsworth (Line 8); free street parking | Hours Daily 8:30am–9:45pm | Tip Continue
supporting local Black businesses by stopping in for a bite at Pizzayaki, a Black-owned
restaurant and lounge that serves pizza and yaki bowls (12544 SE Division Street,
www.pizzayaki.net).

35 _The Green Man of Portland

A "fake legend" based on Old Town's rich history

As the legend goes, when the Green Man pierces you with his arrow, you're forever changed. You begin seeing things you never noticed before: passersby sprout flowers from their heads; a building called The Greenwood appears where no structure stood before; a massive tree towers over the city; on certain nights, a celestial stag gallops in the sky. You have been chosen to perceive the secret history of Portland.

These visions are the premise for Daniel Duford's art installation, *The Green Man of Portland*, which was appropriately selected as part of TriMet's public art display along the MAX Green Line. When the light rail line opened in 2009, TriMet commissioned 40 sculptures from 14 artists to help revitalize the Portland Mall. The idea was for pieces in each region to adhere by a theme, with the North Mall drawing from Old Town/Chinatown's rich history.

When Duford was contacted for the project, he decided to expand on an exhibit he displayed in 2006, *The Green Man of B Street*, which included wall drawings, acrylic paintings, and a 16-page comic. The project consists of two sculptures of the archer and stag and eight "story markers" graphically inspired by '70s horror comics and Work Progress Administration posters, which, together, create a poem. The installation runs throughout 10 blocks of Old Town/Chinatown, along NW 5th and 6th Avenues between Burnside and Glisan Streets. The archer sculpture sits tall at the NW 6th and Davis MAX station, while the stag adorns the NW 5th and Couch stop.

Though only a legend, *The Green Man of Portland* is based on the diverse communities that have called the neighborhood home – from the earliest tribes of the Willamette Valley to contemporary Portlanders. Duford hopes that in time his legend will entwine itself into the fabric of the community's already layered history.

Address Various locations, www.danielduford.com/dana-buckley | **Getting there** A good place to start your journey is at the NW 6th & Davis MAX station, where the archer sculpture is displayed | **Hours** Unrestricted | **Tip** Old Town/Chinatown is budding with art galleries, including the contemporary Froelick Gallery, which is a short walk from the NW 6th & Davis MAX station (714 NW Davis Street, www.froelickgallery.com).

36 _ Grinning Paul Bunyan

A piece of history in Kenton

Like many Portland neighborhoods, Kenton has undergone some drastic changes in recent years. What began as a company town dominated by the meat packing industry in the early 20th century is now a bustling community. The main drag houses a bevy of hip restaurants and boutiques, making it nearly unrecognizable when compared to what it used to be. But as the neighborhood evolves, there's one piece of Kenton that has stayed the same: its beloved Paul Bunyan statue.

The 31-foot-tall statue was erected in 1959 for the Oregon Centennial Exposition and International Trade Fair. Like other depictions of the mythical lumberjack, Paul Bunyan is dressed in a checkered shirt, jeans, and boots, and he wields a monstrous ax. However, there's one characteristic that's unique to Portland's gentle giant: the large grin strewn across his face. It was a fitting touch, considering the sculpture was constructed to welcome visitors to the exposition.

Paul Bunyan's statue was only supposed to stand for six months, but he quickly became a permanent part of Kenton, representing the neighborhood's rugged, working-class spirit. In the years that followed, the statue began to deteriorate and was thoughtfully restored time and time again. In 2002, with the completion of TriMet's MAX Yellow Line, the large figure was moved from his original location on N Argyle and Interstate Avenue to his current home on the corner of N Denver and Interstate – a whopping 59.2 feet away. The relocation didn't seem to bother the lumberjack though, whose kindhearted smile remained plastered on his face.

In 2009, Paul Bunyan was added to the National Register of Historic Places, making him Oregon's only roadside attraction on the register. The statue's latest touchup came in 2017, and he currently resides in his own plaza, standing tall in front of a sign welcoming guests to *Historic Kenton*.

Address N Denver Avenue & Interstate Avenue, Portland, OR 97217 | Getting there
MAX to Kenton/N Denver Avenue (Yellow & Blue Lines); free street parking | Hours
Unrestricted | Tip Are you missing Babe the big blue ox? Look across N Denver Avenue.
There, you'll see four large, blue hooves representing Paul's animal companion.

37 — Hallock-McMillan Building

Portland's oldest surviving commercial building

The mid-19th century was a time of change in the Oregon territory. As the urban center began to shift from Oregon City to Portland, business moved along with it, and by the early 1850s brick commercial buildings began popping up along the waterfront.

In 1857, Absalom Barrett Hallock, the city's first established professional architect, built his firm's headquarters with contractor William McMillan on the corner of SW Front (now Naito Parkway) and Oak. Though a modest, two-story structure, the Hallock-McMillan building was praised for its Greek Revival style and innovative cast-iron facade. It's credited for beginning the Skidmore/Old Town district's period of significance. As Portland solidified its dominance as the Northwest's primary urban center due to its trade-centered economy, Skidmore/Old Town became the city's commercial core – and this was all before Oregon entered statehood in 1859.

As Portland grew away from the waterfront, many of the Skidmore/Old Town buildings were eventually demolished. However, the Hallock-McMillan survived and is now the oldest known commercial building in the city. In the 1940s, the edifice was stripped of its cast-iron work in an effort to "modernize" it, and in 1975 it was listed as a "primary landmark" in the National Register of Historic Places. For decades, the historic yet drab building housed an array of businesses. In 2010, local developer John Russell purchased the property with the plan to restore it to its original glory.

Russell recruited a preservation architectural firm that thoughtfully studied the building's original design and recreated it using materials and methods common to the times. Today you can marvel at its brick exterior, cast-iron archways, and carefully detailed leaf and floral accents – just as they were in 1857.

Address 237 SW Naito Parkway, Portland, OR 97204 | Getting there TriMet to SW Oak & 1st (Line 16); metered street parking | Hours Unrestricted | Tip The Hallock-McMillan building's next-door neighbor, the Fechheimer & White building, was built in 1885 and is one of the finest examples of cast-iron architecture remaining in Portland today (233 SW Naito Parkway).

38__Hip Chicks Do Wine
"Serious wine. Serious fun."

Laurie Lewis and Renee Neely have always been avid wine drinkers, and in the mid-1990s they decided to take that passion to the next level. The couple took winemaking classes and secured jobs at Willamette Valley wineries in an effort to further educate themselves. Their efforts paid off. In 1999, they cashed in their retirement funds, took out a second mortgage on their house, and made 500 cases of wine under the label Hip Chicks Do Wine.

Instead of opening another winery in the Willamette Valley, Lewis and Neely wanted to create something more accessible to Portlanders. In 2001, they opened a tasting room inside their production warehouse tucked between the Brooklyn and Reed neighborhoods. Though the industrial area seems like an odd place to open a winery, Lewis recalls a story from the 1940s of locals purchasing grapes off California trains stopped at the nearby Brooklyn train yards to make basement wine. To her, it was only fitting to open Portland's first urban winery in this locale.

Now urban wineries are thriving in the Rose City, with dozens of winemakers opening facilities within city limits. The pioneering Hip Chicks welcome good competition and have upped their production significantly since their first batch, making reds, whites, and blends from Oregon- and Washington-sourced grapes, as well as starting a reserve label named after their son, Tiernan Connor. In addition to a laid-back wine-tasting atmosphere, Lewis and Neely also host a number of quirky events throughout the year, pairing wines with everything from Girl Scout cookies to bacon.

At Hip Chicks Do Wine, the motto is "Serious Wine. Serious fun. An urban winery for everyone," and boy do they live up to it. "Wine is something that you can get really serious about, and there's nothing wrong with that," Lewis explains. "But at the same time, you can kick back and have some fun with it."

Address 4510 SE 23rd Avenue, Portland, OR 97202, +1 (503) 234-3790, www.hipchicksdowine.com, winegoddess@hipchicksdowine.com | Getting there TriMet to SE 28th & Raymond (Line 10), free parking | Hours Mon 11am–5pm, Tue & Wed 2–6pm, Thu & Sun 11am–6pm, Fri & Sat 11am–7pm | Tip Hop across the river and visit A Yen For Chocolate, the local chocolatier that produces Hip Chicks Do Wine's fabulous port-infused truffles (915 NW 19th Avenue, Suite B, www.ayenforchocolate.com).

39 Hippo Hardware

One person's trash is another person's treasure

Steven Miller and Stephen Oppenheim prefer the love-it-or-hate-it process when it comes to purchasing antique pieces. If an object elicits a strong emotion either way, they take it. If it's just "meh," they move on. "If you *hate* it, someone else is going to love it just as much as you dislike it," Miller explains. "Most people in the antique business buy it if they like it, but I believe that I only represent a small percentage of perspective."

The business partners founded Hippo Hardware in 1976 and have been offering hardware, lighting, architectural details, and plumbing dating between 1860 and 1960 – as well as a collection of whosits and whatsits – to Portland ever since. Through sale and trade, auctions, garage sales, and building demolitions, they've come across solid brass Eastern Griffins, lighting fixtures from a house Frederick Law Olmsted constructed and possibly lived in, and even a box of chastity belts (which they turned down because they didn't have keys). But Miller will tell you what he treasures most.

"A lot of unique pieces come through the door, but the most unique, most valuable, most unusual things are the customers," he says with a smile, sipping coffee from a Hippo Hardware mug. This is how you'll see the eccentric co-owner most days of the week. Now in his 70s, he's on the floor to converse with customers, some of whom he's been serving since before Hippo's inception. The 30,000-square-foot, three-story showroom can be intimidating, but any employee is happy to help you.

"I want to build a life I don't have to take a vacation from, and I want to meet my maker without being terrified," Miller says in a more serious tone. "All of this is part of that pathway. Hippo is all about having fun. Celebrating being alive. Recognizing how special people are – how fragile, how beautiful, how unique. That's really what Hippo's about."

Address 1040 E Burnside Street, Portland, OR 97214, +1 (503) 231-1444, www.hippohardware.com, hippohardware@gmail.com | Getting there TriMet to E Burnside & SE Sandy (Lines 12, 19, & 20); metered and free street parking | Hours Mon–Thu 10am–5pm, Fri & Sat 10am–6pm, Sun noon–5pm | Tip After perusing antique homewares, head down the street to Old Town Music and shop used and vintage music gear (55 SE 11th Avenue, www.oldtownmusicportland.com).

40__Hollywood Theatre

The only place in Portland to see movies in 70mm

When the Hollywood Theatre first opened its doors on July 17, 1926 it was greeted with much fanfare. The goal of the 1,500-seat theater was to transport viewers from the mundane world to an exotic palace of magic and fantasy, and its design mirrored that vision. The intricate Spanish Colonial Revival facade and interior were modeled after the Roman Baths of Caracalla and the 17th-century Italian Basilica of St. Pietro by Lorenzo Bernini. It was the last venue in Portland built as both a Vaudeville house and movie theater, and its silent films were accompanied by an eight-piece orchestra and organist. In fact, Rose City Park residents were so impressed by it that they renamed their neighborhood the Hollywood District.

By 1959, the theater was equipped with 70mm projectors, and in 1961 it became the only Cinerama theater in Oregon. In the 1970s, walls and projection booths were built to divide the balcony, creating three smaller auditoriums, with the main room holding 384 guests. Hollywood was listed in the National Register of Historic Places in 1983, but by then it had fallen into disarray. Nearly 15 years later, the nonprofit Film Action Oregon purchased the struggling theater and restored it to the exotic palace it once was.

Now, the Hollywood Theatre runs as a nonprofit and offers moviegoers experiences they can't find anywhere else. Though it does show digital projections of first-run titles, the theater's main focus is showcasing film. It projects first-run movies in 35mm format whenever possible and is the only theater in Portland that can show movies in 70mm. Aside from new titles, the theater also champions the classics (it has its own 70mm print of *2001: A Space Odyssey*) and hosts a number of monthly events, including Queer Horror, B-Movie Bingo, Kung Fu Theater, and Pipe Organ Pictures, a silent film series accompanied by live organ.

Address 4122 NE Sandy Boulevard, Portland, OR 97212, +1 (503) 493-1128, www.hollywoodtheatre.org, info@hollywoodtheatre.org | Getting there TriMet to NE Sandy & 42nd (Line 12); free street parking | Hours See website for showtimes and events schedule | Tip In 2017, the Hollywood Theatre purchased Movie Madness – a Portland institution since 1991 – and saved the iconic video store from shuttering. Visit the shop to browse its collection of over 80,000 titles and check out some cool film props, including the knife from *Psycho* (4320 SE Belmont Street, www.moviemadness.org).

41 James Beard's Cookbooks

Peep inside a great chef's personal library

James Beard is a revered chef, cookbook author, teacher, and television personality who revolutionized American cuisine. He's also a native Portlander and proud Reed College alumnus (even if he only attended for a semester).

In Fall 1920, Beard (Jimmie, as he was known at school) made quite an impression on the Reed campus. During his short time at the college, Beard was elected as freshman class treasurer, served as anchor of the freshman team in the annual tug-of-war contest (they lost to the sophomores), and, perhaps most memorably, won a Halloween costume contest for dressing in full drag. Though his reason for leaving school abruptly cannot be confirmed (some say he was expelled for poor grades, others that he was expelled for being gay), he was pleased to obtain an honorary degree in 1976.

When he passed away in January 1985, the food aficionado left the bulk of his estate to Reed College, including his personal cookbook collection. The library features books written by Beard (the oldest is a 1949 copy of his fourth work, *The Fireside Cookbook*) and some written by others, like a brittle print of *Peterson's New Cookbook* dating back to 1864. Many of the books are signed or have scribbled notations next to recipes, while some were donated with inserts tucked inside the pages, revealing treasures like handwritten recipes for chow chow relish, notes from friends and colleagues, and bits of ripped up postcards.

Beard's collection is not displayed publicly, but anyone curious to see it may do so at Reed College Library's Special Collections & Archives reading room, located two levels down from the lobby. Upon entering and signing in, you may request any item you'd like to view. The school also offers tours and presentations to groups interested in learning more about the collection, or any of Reed's other special archives, like artist books and calligraphy.

james beard's
treasury of
outdoor
cooking

Address 3203 SE Woodstock Boulevard, Portland, OR 97202, +1 (503) 777-7702, www.library.reed.edu, archives@reed.edu | Getting there TriMet to SE Woodstock & 34th (Line 19); free on-site parking | Hours Mon–Fri 10am–4pm during the school year and by appointment in the summer | Tip While on campus, you can also check out the Reed Research Reactor, the only nuclear reactor operated primarily by undergraduates (www.reactor.reed.edu).

42__Jamison Square Fountain
Splash around in an urban tide pool

There's no better way to beat the summer heat than splashing around in cool water, and though there are plenty of swimming holes along the Willamette and Columbia, taking a dip in the river isn't always the kid-friendliest of options. Thankfully, the city has built a number of splash pads and fountains throughout Portland, including one right in the heart of the Pearl District.

The Jamison Square Fountain was designed to replicate a shallow tide pool. Treated water intermittently cascades over stone joints into a sloped pool, filling up 12 inches before draining back out using energy-efficient pumps. Kids (and adults) of all ages are able to frolic in the cool water as it flows into the pool, while those a little more daring can climb the rocks and play in the waterfalls as they gently descend.

As children splash in the fountain, parents can keep a close eye while lounging on the lush grass surrounding the square. Bring a blanket and a book and catch some rays while the little ones play, or pack a picnic lunch and spend an afternoon in the park.

Jamison Square was named after William Jamison, a late gallery owner who helped create the Pearl District's burgeoning art scene, so it's only fitting that the plaza is edged with four 30-foot sculptures. The *Tikitotemoniki Totems* were constructed by artist Kenny Scharf and transform the streetcar catenary poles into technicolor abstract art. The square also houses a 7-foot metal sculpture built by Alexander Liberman titled *Contact II. Rico Pasado* (which translates to "rich past") is a red granite sculpture created by Mauricio Saldaña and modeled after a brown bear to represent the great wildlife that once roamed this area.

Though the water is turned off in the winter, a large Christmas tree decorates the park during the holidays, giving you a reason to visit Jamison Square all year round.

Address 810 NW 11th Avenue, Portland, OR 97209, +1 (503) 823-7529, www.portlandoregon.gov/parks/finder | **Getting there** Portland Streetcar to NW 11th & Johnson (B Loop & NS Lines) or to NW 10th & Johnson (A Loop & NS Lines); metered street parking | **Hours** Fountain runs daily 8am–10pm except in winter | **Tip** Visit Tanner Springs, a park honoring the Pearl District's wetlands past, just two blocks away (NW 10th Avenue & Marshall Street, www.portlandoregon.gov/parks/finder).

43 __Japanese American Historical Plaza

Commemorating those sent to WWII internment camps

A grove of cherry blossom trees paint Portland's Waterfront Park every spring. The delicate flowers and pastel pinks contrasted with the steely blue of the Willamette River are a breathtaking sight, but they are not simply beautiful. They tell a story.

The trees surround the Japanese American Historical Plaza, a memorial dedicated in 1990 to help spread awareness of the *Nikkei*, Americans of Japanese descent, who were forced from their homes and sent to internment camps during World War II.

The memorial flows south to north, like the Willamette, and it follows an undulating wall of 18 stones and markers. The first stone is an engraved copy of the Bill of Rights, portraying the importance of the Constitution. From there, it tells the story of the *Issei*, Japanese-born immigrants, as they sailed across the Pacific Ocean to plant roots in California, Oregon, and Washington. "Mighty Willamette! Beautiful friend. I am learning. I am practicing to say your name," reads the first poem.

The joy quickly turns to fear as *Nisei*, American-born children of Japanese immigrant parents, are looked at differently at school. And the internments inevitably begin. In the middle, the wall is broken, with a taller stone rising amongst shattered rock. The 10 internment camps are etched here, with the break representing the damage these events caused the *Nikkei*.

Though the internment camps were a shameful blot in American history, the plaza shines a light in the dark. The final poems tell stories of returning to Oregon in the red hue of autumn, and though the old communities no longer exist, the *Nikkei* can hear their echoes. The last stones portray the Civil Liberties Act and Congress' apology to Japanese Americans, a hope that all Americans may always be free.

Address The western entrance just northeast of the corner of NW Naito Parkway and NW Couch Street, +1 (503) 224-1458, www.oregonnikkei.org/plaza.htm | **Getting there** TriMet to NW Naito Parkway & Couch (Line 16); metered street parking | **Hours** Daily 5am–midnight | **Tip** Just a few short blocks from the plaza is the Oregon Nikkei Legacy Center, which houses a museum dedicated to celebrating Japanese Americans (121 NW 2nd Avenue, www.oregonnikkei.org).

44 Kelly Butte Defense Center
Portland's abandoned nuclear bunker

When you first arrive at Kelly Butte Natural Area, it's not uncommon to feel a sense of unease. The main entrance feels a bit strange. You park your car on an access road that's been gated off. The guardrails are covered in graffiti. There's trash scattered on the ground. Rarely are there any other hikers around. You're surrounded by trees and wildlife, and yet it still feels abandoned. And in a way, it is.

Though parts of the area have always been used for recreation, the nearly 23-acre space has housed a quarry, jail, isolation hospital, emergency call center, and currently holds a 25-million-gallon water reservoir. But in the 1950s, the park lived its most bizarre life as the Kelly Butte Civil Defense Center.

At the height of the Cold War, Portland found it necessary to build an underground bunker to shelter government officials in the event of a nuclear attack. The command center was completed in 1956 at a cost of $670,000. The state-of-the-art facility was the first of its kind in the US and was used as a model for other installations. The 18,820-square-foot space was able to house 250 people with enough resources, including purified air and back-up power, to last two weeks. The main purpose was to provide the surviving population with information and coordinated help after a nuclear attack.

In 1957, the center was featured in a dramatized nuclear war documentary titled *A Day Called X*. At the time, it employed seven full-time civil defense workers and a handful of volunteers; however, as the threat of nuclear attack decreased, so did its necessity. By 1968, the bunker only had one part-time employee.

In 2006, the defunct facility was sealed off and covered in dirt. Today, only the top of the concrete building is visible above the landfill, but you can still feel the unsettling energy that emanates from the butte's many past lives.

Address SE 103rd Avenue, Portland, OR 97266, +1 (503) 823-7529, www.portlandoregon.gov/parks/finder | Getting there Free parking near gated-off entrance | Hours Daily 5am–noon | Tip If you're looking for a butte with scenic views and a more peaceful atmosphere, head north to Rocky Butte Natural Area, which boasts views of the Boring Lava Field, Mount St. Helens, and Mount Hood (3102 NE Rocky Butte Road, www.portlandoregon.gov/parks/finder).

45 Ladies of Paradise
Where women fly high

When you walk past the Ladies of Paradise storefront, the sign's neon glow urges visitors to check out what's inside, and the vibrant interior makes it difficult to leave.

Upon entering, it feels like a typical boutique. Tables of trinkets welcome you. Clothes hang on display, begging to be worn. There are hats, jewelry, bath salts, and lots of pink items. But when you look to the back of the store, you realize the wallpaper's green foliage isn't palm fronds. It's marijuana leafs. You're in a weed shop.

When Harlee Case and Jade Daniels decided to open Ladies of Paradise, their goal was to change the cannabis industry for the better. Their store champions female artists, designers, and cannabis connoisseurs, with the majority of their weed-centric accessories, clothing, housewares, and CBD products made by women-owned brands, like Blunted Objects, Vida Kush, High Society Collection, 2Rise Naturals, Wildflower, and AllayTopicals. "Customers often hang out on our sofa and stick around for the vibes," Daniels explains. "And so many women who come in end up leaving as friends."

But the brick and mortar is only a small part of Case and Daniel's vision. Aside from the boutique, Ladies of Paradise is also a branding and marketing firm, a cannabis-consumption event planning company, and, after launching their Lady Jays pre-rolls in 2019, a product line. While feminism is at the heart of everything the team of women does, they're also interested in reversing the stigma that's typically associated with consuming marijuana. Their parties are creative and fun; their photo shoots are tasteful and editorially driven, and their products are thoughtfully and vibrantly packaged. But most of all, they're inclusive and conscientious about everything they do. Ladies of Paradise is a place where women can fly high, even if they don't partake in cannabis consumption.

Address 959 SE Division Street, Suite 125, Portland, OR 97214, www.ladiesofparadise.com, contact@ladiesofparadise.com | **Getting there** TriMct to SE Division Place & 8th (Line 9 & 17); free street parking | **Hours** Tue–Sat 11am–6pm, Sun 1–6pm | **Tip** Ladies of Paradise shares a building with some other fabulous companies, including the vibrant Cuban bar Palomar (959 SE Division Street, Suite 100, www.barpalomar.com).

46__Lan Su Chinese Garden

An homage to Portland's sister city Suzhou

In 1988, Suzhou became Portland's Chinese sister city, and on September 14, 2000, the Lan Su Chinese Garden opened in Portland's Old Town/Chinatown neighborhood. The walled garden represents the two cities' special relationship and is poetically interpreted as "Garden of the Awakening Orchids."

The Chinese city is known for its gardens, and over the course of nine months, more than 60 Suzhou craftsmen meticulously landscaped the 40,000-square-foot space to replicate the traditional gardens that have flourished in their homeland for thousands of years. Among the native materials imported to create Lan Su, the Lake Tai rocks may be most impressive. More than 600 tons of the uniquely shaped stones were shipped to Portland and have been designed to appear as rugged mountain tops.

Those who visit the Chinese Garden are treated to a tranquil reprieve from the bustling city right outside its walls. Lan Su embodies the harmony of Yin and Yang – light and shadows; water and stone; sky and earth, all while soaring buildings juxtapose the delicate landscape of the garden. Hundreds of plant species grow within Lan Su's walls, and roughly 90 percent are indigenous to China. The garden's pavilions and vista points center around the manmade Zither Lake, brimming with koi fish, while each structure tells an important story of Chinese culture. The on-site teahouse allows guests to enjoy traditional tea ceremonies and authentic fare, such as mooncakes and steamed buns.

No Chinese Garden is complete without poetry, and beautiful words are inscribed throughout Lan Su. In the Flowers Bathing in Spring Rain Pavilion, you'll find these fitting words from ancient Chinese scholar Wen Zhengming etched on the fourth of six panels: *Most cherished in this mundane world is a place without traffic; Truly in the midst of the city there can be mountain and forest.*

Address 239 NW Everett Street, Portland, OR 97209, +1 (503) 228-8131, www.lansugarden.org, info@lansugarden.org | Getting there TriMet to NW Everett & 2nd (Lines 4, 8, 16, 35, 44, & 77); MAX to Old Town/Chinatown (Red & Blue Lines); metered street parking | Hours Daily 10am–6pm | Tip Right down the street, you can learn about the area's past, present, and future at the Portland Chinatown Museum (127 NW 3rd Avenue, www.portlandchinatownmuseum.org).

47__The Loaded Brush
Sip (or puff) and paint

When Aaron Ziobrowski moved to Portland in 2008, it was with the intention of starting his own art studio. Then he went to a sip-n-paint class while visiting his family in Atlanta, and everything changed. He found the event's vibe to be painfully corporate, with 60 patrons being taught by a fresh-out-of-high-school instructor. Yet everyone seemed to have a great time.

"I thought to myself if beginners are having this good of a time making art and it's a pretty cheesy environment, just imagine how much fun they would have if I ran smaller class sizes and actually put some instructional love into it," Ziobrowski recalls. This revelation was the impetus for The Loaded Brush and why it thrives amidst competition from other local sip-n-paint studios.

Ziobrowski and a team of enthusiastic, knowledgeable instructors teach classes that range from five to twenty people. The intimate setting allows them to be more hands-on with students as they teach step-by-step tutorials on how to paint everything from Multnomah Falls to Van Gogh's *Starry Night*. The Loaded Brush provides everything you might need for a successful painting (easel, canvas, brushes, paint, smocks, and, of course, alcohol).

Wine goes for $6 a glass, while beer and cider can be purchased for $5. There are also non-alcoholic options for those who'd prefer to paint with a clear mind. Students are welcome to BYOB, though a $10 corkage fee is charged per party. The studio also occasionally teams up with local cannabis clubs to offer Puff-n-Paint, which is the same concept as a sip-n-paint, but with weed.

Aside from the standard acrylic and watercolor classes, The Loaded Brush also hosts private parties and Paint Your Pet events, which is more of a 'paint by number' format. First time painting? Don't worry – every class is geared towards beginners and structured to ensure a good time is had by all.

Address 5538 SE 22nd Avenue, Portland, OR 97202, +1 (503) 468-5057, www.loadedbrushpdx.com, the.loaded.helpdesk@gmail.com | **Getting there** TriMet to SE Milwaukie & Insley (Line 19); small on-site parking lot and free street parking | **Hours** See website for class schedule | **Tip** For a post-painting nightcap, grab a beer at the nearby Gigantic Brewing Company (5224 SE 26th Avenue, www.giganticbrewing.com).

48___Lownsdale Square
A pickup site for "immoral" activity

Chapman and Lownsdale Squares comprise the Plaza Blocks in bustling Southwest Portland. Divided by the historic *Elk* statue in the middle of Main Street, these two public parks welcome anyone who wants to have a picnic in the grass, read a book on a bench, or simply take a stroll along their paved paths. But that wasn't always the case. When the Plaza Blocks were acquired in the late 19th century, Chapman was designed for the exclusive use of women and children, while Lownsdale was to be a "gentlemen's gathering place." That place of congregation would later be a site of one of the city's most notorious scandals.

On November 8, 1912, a wayward 19-year-old named Benjamin Trout was arrested for petty crimes. During his interrogation, the teen exposed sensational details about local homosexual activity happening throughout the city. At the time, gay subculture was forced underground and authorities were outraged to hear that men – many of them prominent in society – were engaging in such dubious acts. Of the many pickup sites listed was Lownsdale Square.

Over 60 men would end up being arrested and charged with crimes ranging from indecent acts to sodomy in what is now known as the Portland Vice Scandal (or Vice Clique Scandal). The scandal consumed newspaper headlines for weeks, but its impact would last decades. Though most involved had charges dropped for lack of corroborating evidence, at least seven men were convicted or plead guilty. Many were shamed out of their careers and shunned from the city. At least one of the implicated men attempted suicide. The scandal led states throughout the Northwest to strengthen sodomy laws and go so far as to implement eugenics programs to sterilize sex offenders.

Though Portland is now one of the most welcoming cities to the LGBTQ+ community, it's important to remember that it hasn't always been that way.

Address SW 4th Avenue and Main Street, Portland, OR 97204, +1 (503) 823-7529, www.portlandoregon.gov/parks | Getting there MAX to City Hall/SW 5th & Jefferson (Green & Orange Lines); TriMet to SW 3rd & Madison (Line 6); metered parking | Hours Daily 5am–midnight | Tip Visit the Portland Police Museum and Historical Society just down the street from Lownsdale Square (1111 SW 2nd Avenue, www.portlandpolicemuseum.com).

49 Loyal Legion
Ninety-nine problems, but a beer ain't one

In 1908, the International Organization Of Odd Fellows opened its Orient Lodge #17 on SE 6th and Alder, which acted as the fraternity's meeting hall for half a century. The Portland Police Athletic Association (PPAA) bought the building in the 1950s, transforming the upper level into an event space and members-only bar that infamously got so rowdy, the Portland Police had to crack down on its own people in the 1990s. The ground floor housed a rotating cast of businesses, including The Office Supply Co. and Citizen's Photo. The PPAA sold the building in 2013, as many of the city's historic structures were shuttering.

In an effort to preserve Old Portland in a time of great change, restaurant group ChefStable bought the property and opened a beer hall dedicated to Oregon brewers. They called it Loyal Legion. Years before pouring their first beer, ChefStable owner Kurt Huffman stumbled upon a sign in the basement of an old building when he was constructing his first Portland restaurant that read, 'Loyal Legion of Loggers and Lumbermen Employment Services'. The sheet metal plaque now hangs with pride in the bar as another reminder of the city's rich history.

When the beer hall opened in 2015, it offered 99 Oregon brews on tap and a limited food menu. Though beer is still its primary offering, the well-stocked bar now offers 250 whiskeys, 150 other spirits, a full cocktail program, and ample food options prepared by Chef Liz Serrone.

But perhaps more impressive than Loyal Legion's plethora of choices is its staff. In an effort to educate guests to their full potential, every bartender must be Cicerone-certified (the beer equivalent to a sommelier). With such an extensive menu – Loyal Legion is the biggest provider of tapped Oregon beer, period – the bar is dedicated to helping patrons find their favorite local brew. Cheers to that.

Address 710 SE 6th Avenue, Portland, OR 97214, +1 (503) 235-8272, www.loyallegionpdx.com, info@loyallegionpdx.com | Getting there Portland Streetcar to SE Grand & Belmont (B Loop); TriMet to SE Grand & Belmont (Line 6); metered street parking | Hours Sun–Thu 11:30am–midnight, Fri & Sat 11:30–2am | Tip Whiskey connoisseurs will take particular delight in the collection Multnomah Whiskey Library has to offer (1124 SW Alder Street, www.mwlpdx.com).

50__The Martha Washington

An attack that led the Rajneeshee to militancy

The Martha Washington building has lived many lives. It opened in 1917 as a residence for young single women. Today, it's publicly subsidized affordable housing. But perhaps its most interesting (and notorious) incarnation is what it became in between.

When Netflix released *Wild, Wild Country* in 2018, the world learned about the free-love-promoting guru Bhagwan Shree Rajneesh and his group of followers. Though much of the story takes place in Eastern Oregon, the event that possibly tipped the Rajneeshee from love to violence occurred in Portland. In January 1983 the Rajneesh Investment Corporation (RIC) bought the Martha Washington and transformed it into Hotel Rajneesh. Just months later, on July 29, 1983, three small bombs went off in the 127-room building. The first exploded at 1:22am and blew a hole in the bathroom wall of Room 405. The other two detonated around an hour later, both hidden under the room's beds.

A man named Stephen P. Paster carried out the attack with no known motive and lost a few fingers in the initial blast. Once convicted, he spent five years in the Oregon State Penitentiary. Though Paster was the only person injured in the bombing, the Rajneeshee purchased a cache of guns in its wake and began target-shooting practice at their headquarters, a sprawling ranch in Wasco County. The religious group also launched a private security operation, complete with automatic weapon-wielding guards.

The commune would eventually collapse under the weight of murder plots, wiretapping scandals, and other dubious offenses by its leadership. More than two dozen people were convicted or implicated in illegal activity, and Bhagwan was deported in 1985. A year later, RIC sold the building to Multnomah County. In 2010, it reopened as the Martha Washington Apartments, but it will forever be infamously remembered as Hotel Rajneesh.

Address 1115 SW 11th Avenue, Portland, OR 97205, +1 (503) 525-8483 | Getting there TriMet to SW Salmon & 12th (Lines 15 & 51); Portland Streetcar to SW 11th & Jefferson (B Loop & NS Lines); metered street parking | Hours Unrestricted | Tip Continue your Rajneesh tour of Portland by visiting Southpark Seafood just a few blocks away. The restaurant used to be the site of the RIC-owned Zorba the Buddha Nightclub & Restaurant (901 SW Salmon Street, www.southparkseafood.com).

51 McLoughlin House
Home of the "Father of Oregon"

John McLoughlin crossed the Rockies in 1824 as chief factor of the British Hudson's Bay Company (HBC). The Canadian-born businessman was sent to the area to establish the company's Columbia Department headquarters and a year later founded Fort Vancouver. When American pioneers began crossing the Oregon Trail in the early 1840s, McLoughlin was told to turn them away when they reached the fort, but he didn't have the heart. Instead he allowed them to retrieve supplies from the warehouse on credit, which eventually cost him his job.

While scouting for HBC, McLoughlin came across Willamette Falls and founded what is now Oregon City in 1929 to take advantage of the falls' power and run a lumber mill. After losing his job, McLoughlin was forced to purchase the land he had claimed for the company. He built a house near the falls, and in 1846 he and his wife Marguerite moved in. McLoughlin thrived in Oregon City, opening a mercantile that served pioneers fresh off the Oregon Trail and briefly serving as mayor. In 1851, he officially became a US citizen. John and Marguerite lived in their Georgian-style home until their deaths in 1857 and 1860, respectively. In 1910, the historic house was moved to its current site in the heart of Oregon City.

Because of his significant role in the state's early history, McLoughlin is known as the Father of Oregon, and his famous house is open to the public free of charge. Enthusiastic tour guides tell McLoughlin's story in interactive ways before leading visitors into the house. Once inside, you can view the fully furnished parlor, office, sewing room, dining room, and four bedrooms that make up the two-story, 2,500-square-foot home. All the décor is era-appropriate, and roughly one-third of the collection is original to the home. While you're there, you can visit John and Marguerite, who are buried just outside the house.

Address 713 Centre Street, Oregon City, OR 97045, +1 (503) 656-5146, www.mcloughlinhouse.org, mcloughlinmemorial@gmail.com | Getting there Free street parking | Hours Feb–Dec; tours Fri & Sat 10am–4pm | Tip The tours begin in the Barclay House, which is also worth a visit, as it is quite rich in Oregon history (719 Center Street, Oregon City, OR 97045, www.mcloughlinhouse.org/the-barclay-house.html).

52 McMenamins Kennedy School

School's out forever

Kennedy School is rooted in Portland's Concordia neighborhood, tucked away from the local boutiques, trendy bars and restaurants that swarm the city's east side. When the first bell rang in 1915, the elementary school stood three blocks past the nearest streetcar stop. It was just eight blocks away from the city line, and the students that resided beyond NE 42nd Avenue lived without water and electricity.

As the years passed, the city grew up around the schoolhouse. The neighborhood began to flourish, and Kennedy School became a public meeting and polling place, as well as serving other civic roles. It was a community hub for decades. But in the mid-1970s everything changed. The 1974–75 school year proved to be a difficult one for Portland. Enrollment began to decline districtwide, and the 60-year-old building was declared dilapidated beyond repair. At the end of the school year, Kennedy Elementary closed its doors for good.

Over 20 years later, the city approved the McMenamin brothers' proposal to rejuvenate life into the condemned building by converting it into one of their revered hotels and pubs. On October 22, 1997, the original principal's bell rang, signifying a new era in the school's storied history.

The cafeteria may now be a restaurant, and the common areas include bars, gift shops, soaking pools, a brewery, and a movie theater, but Kennedy School's spirit has been preserved. Its walls are covered in murals that tell the stories of past students and teachers, and the hotel houses 57 guest rooms with a wing fashioned from former classrooms – chalkboard, cloakroom, and all. Patrons can explore the school's boiler room in its new form, a multilevel bar. Troublemakers can drink McMenamins-brewed beer at the Detention Bar, while straight-A students sip premium cocktails in the Honors Bar.

Address 5736 NE 33rd Avenue, Portland, OR 97211, +1 (503) 249-3983,
www.mcmenamins.com/kennedy-school, generalinfo@mcmenamins.com | **Getting there**
TriMet to NE 33rd & Jarrett (Line 70); free street parking | **Hours** See website for special
tours | **Tip** For more McMenamins magic, visit the nearby Chapel Pub. The restaurant/bar
is housed in the renovated Little Chapel of the Chimes, which was built in 1932
(430 N Killingsworth Street, www.mcmenamins.com/chapel-pub).

53__Merchants' Hotel

A Portland fixture since the 1880s

Portland in the 19th century was much like the Wild, Wild West. Many "residents" were transient men working in Northwest lumber camps, and brothels, opium dens, saloons, and gambling halls were abundant in the port town. However, as the city's population grew, so did its economy, and by the latter part of the century, an influx of legitimate businesses began to open. During this era, a number of solid lodging structures were also built, including the Merchants' Hotel.

When it opened in the mid-1880s, the Merchant was considered one of the finest hotels in the city and was lauded for having one of Portland's first hydraulic elevators. Aside from guest accommodations, it's also housed a variety of retail businesses that included a dance hall, a billiard room, and a cracker company over the years.

From around 1904 until the mid-1940s, the Merchant was a central fixture to Portland's Japantown. During this time a number of Japanese businesses, from specialized grocery and dry goods shops to the offices of local Japanese newspaper *Oshu Nippo*, resided in the building. The Oregon Nikkei Legacy Center, an organization and museum dedicated to celebrating Japanese-American culture, currently calls the Merchant home.

Today, the Merchant is one of the few remaining examples of Victorian Italianate, cast-iron architecture on the West Coast. It was listed on the US National Register of Historic Places in 1975 and deemed a National Historic Landmark District two years later.

There is one long-time resident who has never left. Portland's most famous ghost Nina is said to haunt Old Town Pizza & Brewing in the building. As the legend goes, Nina was a prostitute who was thrown down the elevator shaft. She's said to haunt the basement, where people have reported hearing breathing, smelling perfume, feeling a tap on their shoulder, and seeing a woman in a black dress.

Address 121 NW Second Avenue, Portland, OR 97209 | Getting there MAX to Old Town/Chinatown (Red & Blue Lines); TriMet to West Burnside & NW 2nd (Lines 12, 19, & 20); metered street parking | Hours Unrestricted | Tip Learn more about Nina's tragic story during a tour of the Shanghai Tunnels, which happens to begin at the Merchants' Hotel (www.portlandtunnels.com).

54_Mill Ends Park

The only leprechaun colony west of Ireland

When you arrive at 56 SW Taylor Street, you might be a little confused. You could swear this was the address for Mill Ends Park, but all you see is a parking management center. Could you have misread the address? A park should be easy to spot, right? Wrong. Turn so you're facing Naito Parkway. See that crosswalk? Begin crossing until you've reached the middle of Naito. Look down. You've arrived at Mill Ends Park.

In 1946, after fighting in World War II, Dick Fagan returned home to Portland and resumed his journalism career at *The Oregon Journal*. From his office window, Fagan noticed a hole in a median meant for a light pole that never arrived. The writer got sick of seeing the two-foot-wide plot collect weeds and decided to plant flowers. On March 17, 1948 (St. Patrick's Day), the Irishman dedicated his tiny park. He named it after his "Mill Ends" column in the *Journal* and often wrote fantastical articles about its unusual inhabitants: a colony of leprechauns.

His favorite character was the community's leader, Patrick O'Toole, who once published a not-so-favorable response when the mayor tried to enforce an 11pm curfew on city parks. And if you asked Fagan about his park's origin, he'd tell you a fine story. From his office window, he spotted a leprechaun digging in the median hole. He ran down and caught the little fella, who granted him a wish. Fagan wished for a park of his own, but because he never specified a size, he was left with a 452-square-inch plot in the middle of a busy street.

Fagan died of cancer in 1969, but his spirit lives on. In 1971, *The Guinness Book of World Records* named Mill Ends Park the smallest park in the world, and on March 17, 1976, it was declared an official park. Today, its inhabitants are a rotating variety of small trees, shrubs, flowers, and rocks. But if you look closely, you might just see a leprechaun.

Address 56 SW Taylor Street, Portland, OR 97204, +1 (503) 823-7529, www.portlandoregon.gov/parks/finder | **Getting there** MAX to Yamhill District (Red & Blue Lines); metered street parking | **Hours** Unrestricted | **Tip** Take a stroll in the nearby Tom McCall Waterfront Park, which stretches across the western side of the Willamette River (Naito Parkway between SW Harrison and NW Glisan Street, www.portlandoregon.gov/parks/finder).

55 Monticello Antique Market
Stuffy antique shop, this is not

When Kelli Vinther opened the Monticello Antique Marketplace in 1999, she'll be the first to admit she didn't know what she was doing. At the time, antiquing was a hobby, but most local shops she visited felt dingy.

"I thought, *I could do this better*," she says with a laugh.

When she first opened the doors to the 26,000-square-foot emporium, she had 10 vendors. As the space filled up, the proprietress began weeding out dealers that either didn't carry the right kinds of merchandise ("I didn't open this place to sell Beanie Babies!") or weren't bringing in enough sales. Now, the antique mall houses upwards of 90 quality stalls, each acting as a time machine to eras past. She also runs a consignment warehouse, showroom, and café.

As the items change, so do the displays, allowing for a different shopping experience with each visit. Vinther explains that to many, a walk through the aisles is a form of therapy. Teachers come to catch their breath; employees from neighboring businesses spend their lunch breaks; retirees frequently come in and browse.

The staff also encourages "sipping and shopping." Monti's café serves beer and wine, which can be enjoyed while perusing, as well as a full breakfast and lunch menu filled with decadent, homemade fare. While you'll see Vinther walking the grounds or manning the cash register most days, she's also dedicated herself two days off a week, a feat not many small business owners can pull off. But it's all thanks to a well-cultivated team and confidence in her vision. In fact, she encourages dealers to sell to other shops.

"I'm not afraid of competition," Vinther declares. "I think there's room enough for everybody."

It's an easy sentiment to have when you run such a joyous business. This isn't a stuffy antique store. It's a trove of reasonably priced treasure curated by a team that feels like family.

Address 8600 SE Stark Street, Portland, OR 97216, +1 (503) 256-8600, www.monticelloantiques.com | Getting there TriMet to SE Washington & 86th (Line 15); free street parking | Hours Mon–Sat 10am–6pm, Sun 10am–5pm | Tip If you're on the hunt for vintage furniture, after you stroll through Monticello Antique Marketplace, try your luck at Lounge Lizard (1310 SE Hawthorne Boulevard, www.pdxloungelizard.com).

56 Moonshadow Magick

Portland's oldest Pagan resource

Debora Lakey was born with an innate knowledge of herbs. She couldn't name specific plants or their medicinal properties, but she intuitively knew how different spices and herbs affected the body.

"I believe in reincarnation," she explains. "I think I was an herbalist in a past life. I didn't remember the specifics about the herbs – I just knew."

In her 20s, Debora began studying herbalism, and her fascination grew to the point that she wanted her own store. In the summer of 1995, Debora and her husband Roland opened Moonshadow Magick Pagan Shoppe on Hawthorne. They sold 15 types of herbs and a handful of other pagan tools.

As their clientele increased, so did their inventory. They eventually outgrew the store and moved Moonshadow to its current location on Belmont. Though still specializing in herbs – they offer 200 different kinds – the couple's main goal is to offer pagan resources for prayer work and magick. They provide tarot, candles, crystals, stones, statues, oils, and various other tools used in numerous forms of paganism including Wiccan, Druid, and Celtic, among others.

The store itself has a calming energy. The smell of incense is intoxicating, as soothing music plays from the speakers. Debora is happy to answer any questions patrons may have about her products and provides reference books for those who'd like to do their own research.

In fact, Debora is still learning every day. She tells a story about a cut on her finger that wouldn't heal. One day, she was arbitrarily playing with a piece of rhodonite and soon realized her finger had stopped throbbing. Later, she read that the stone helps with inflammation.

"Stones aren't just rocks," she says. "I think they're gifts given to us by the god and the goddess to bring us happiness and healing." Moonshadow is her way to share her energy and offer those gifts and knowledge to others.

Address 3819 SE Belmont Street, Portland, OR 97214, +1 (503) 235-5774, www.moonshadowmagick.com, shop@moonshadowmagick.com | Getting there TriMet to SE Belmont & 37th (Line 15); free street parking | Hours Mon–Wed & Fri & Sat noon–6pm, Sun noon–5pm | Tip Visit Anjali Healing Center to continue uplifting the Spirit, Body, and Mind (3430 SE Belmont Street, www.anjalihealingcenter.com).

57__The Morrison Street Minigallery

Bigger isn't always better

The Morrison Street Minigallery is nothing like you've ever seen before. In fact, you may not see it at all when you first arrive. You gaze up at a beautiful 19th-century Victorian house, but it doesn't look like a place of business. Did you get the address wrong? As you get closer, you notice a small, backlit box to the left of the staircase. That's it. You're at the gallery.

Alissa and Jerry Tran are fascinated with the abundance of mini libraries in Portland, and Alissa, an art teacher who was raised by art teachers, loved the idea of making art just as accessible to the community. She nonchalantly mentioned this to her husband, and the next thing she knew, he had built a tiny gallery in their front yard.

That was in 2017. Since then, they've switched out shows every month. Alissa creates most of the exhibits, using materials like paint, ceramics, clay, fabric, metal, and beads to build tableaus that range from *X-Files* homages to the bedroom of an angsty teenage anglerfish named Keith.

"It started as a fun pet project that we hoped would make people smile, and I think we can say that it's done that," Alissa says with pride. "But it's interesting to see that it has taken off."

As word has spread, the Trans have been able to recruit local artists for guest shows. They've also kept it in the family, running a one-day show produced by their nieces and garden party diorama by Alissa's mom to celebrate Mother's Day.

"We really hope this is something that will spread, and that maybe it will inspire other people to go do other random, creative acts of kindness," Alissa explains. "There are lots of ways for people to engage with the arts that don't have to be expensive and don't have to be exclusive.

Address 3229 SE Morrison Street, Portland, OR 97214, www.sites.google.com/site/morrisonstreetminigallery/home, morrisonstreetminigallery@gmail.com | **Getting there** TriMet to SE Belmont & 34th (Line 15); free street parking | **Hours** Unrestricted | **Tip** The Trans are big fans of the nature-focused Antler Gallery in the Alberta Arts District (2728 NE Alberta Street, www.antlerpdx.com).

The Morrison Street Minigallery
est. 2017

58__Mount Tabor

A dormant volcano in the city

Portland is one of only four cities in the United States to house a dormant volcano within its boundaries. That's one bit of information a Friends of Mount Tabor Park volunteer will tell you when you drop into the Visitors Center. On any given day, visitors are greeted by one of the park's many loyal helpers, and today it's Randy Lawler and his "ferocious guard dog" Allie, a spunky 15-month-old Anatolian Shepherd.

The retired truck driver has been fascinated by the 636-foot cinder cone and the park's rich history since he began volunteering in 2017. He points out a poster of Israel's Mount Tabor, the volcano's namesake, tacked on the wall and explains how Plympton Kelly, son of Oregon City pioneer Clinton Kelly, thought up the name in the mid-1800s. He talks about the seven water reservoirs built in the park at the turn of the 20th century, and how all but one have since been buried or decommissioned. He boasts that Gutzon Borglum, the sculptor famous for designing Mount Rushmore, created a bronze statue of the famed *Oregonian* editor Harvey W. Scott in 1933, and how Mount Tabor is home to two of the city's Heritage Trees: the Bigleaf Linden and Giant Sequoia, both located near Reservoir 6.

As he passionately details the park's current features – a network of trails, three playgrounds, the caldera amphitheater, numerous wedding sites – a regular swings by with her dog. Randy greets the animal by name, Dingo, and opens his desk drawer to reveal a box of milk bones. After giving one to both Dingo and Allie, his eyes light up as he discusses his favorite part of Mount Tabor: the off-leash dog area that he and Allie will enjoy after his shift.

"People have told me I should write a book about Mount Tabor," Randy says. And he should. But until then, he's happy to give an oral history to anyone who'd like to stop by the visitors center and say hi.

Address 6000 SE Salmon Street, Portland, Oregon 97215, +1 (503) 512-0816, www.taborfriends.org, taborfriends@gmail.com | **Getting there** TriMet to SE 69th & Yamhill Street (Line 15); free on-site parking lot | **Hours** Daily 5am–midnight | **Tip** After a nice hike in the park, treat yourself to some of the best pizza in town at the nearby Apizza Scholls (4741 SE Hawthorne Boulevard, www.apizzascholls.com).

59 Mt. Scott Indoor Pool

Splish splash in the dead of winter

As soon as the sun begins to shine and the temperature rises past 70 degrees, it's officially summer in Portland. Locals flock to their favorite swimming holes, urban beaches, splash pads, and outdoor swimming pools. But what about the nine months out of the year where the weather's a little touch-and-go (or downright atrocious)? Thankfully, the city offers a number of indoor facilities to satisfy avid swimmers (and parents of energetic children) during the dreary months, like the Mt. Scott Community Center & Indoor Pool.

The community center pool has been serving members of the Mt. Scott neighborhood and anyone else wanting to swim in SE Portland since 1927, and the community center received a major facelift, including a new pool, in 2000. Now, the amenities include a six-lane, 25-yard lap pool, whirlpool spa heated at 102 degrees, and a leisure pool for the little ones with depths ranging from zero to three-and-a-half feet. The leisure pool is full of activities for kids. Young ones can splash in the play fountain or float around the lazy river (just watch out for that central vortex), while older children spin down the spiral-shaped water slide. Aside from open and lap swim, the Mt. Scott pool offers everything from swimming lessons and parent/preschool swim to Aquaerobics and Aqua Zumba.

In addition to the year-round pool, Mt. Scott Community Center also boasts a fitness center, gymnasium, traverse climbing wall, auditorium, adult and youth fitness classes, preschool program, reservable meeting and party rooms, and even a roller rink, offering Portlanders plenty of indoor activities during the winter months. Though the drop-in admission rate is reasonable, 20-punch and monthly pass options are encouraged for those visiting the community center regularly. City of Portland residents also benefit from discounted rates on all fee tiers.

Address 5530 SE 72nd Avenue, Portland, OR 97206, +1 (503) 823-3183, www.portlandoregon.gov/parks/finder | Getting there TriMet to SE Harold & 72nd (Line 10); free on-site parking lot | Hours Mon–Fri 5:30am–9:30pm, Sat 7am–7pm, Sun noon–7pm | Tip When the weather is nice, enjoy neighboring Mt. Scott Park's 11 acres of trees and recreational facilities, including a playground, horseshoe pit, picnic area, tennis court, and softball field (SE 72nd Avenue & SE Harold Street).

60__Music Millennium
The birthplace of "Keep Portland Weird"

Music Millennium has been an audiophile haven since 1969, making it the oldest continually existing record store in the Pacific Northwest. In its 50-plus years, the record store has hosted thousands of in-store performances, including Soundgarden's *Louder Than Love* release in 1989, and been a must-visit for actors like Helena Bonham Carter and Benicio Del Toro while filming in town. But like any business, it's had its ups and downs. Thankfully, it's owned by Terry Currier. And he won't let it die.

He laments the number of record stores in America dwindling from 7,500 in 2000 to 1,800 in 2007 as the industry shifted to digital formats. In order to ensure his store didn't end up a statistic, he founded the Coalition of Independent Music Stores (CIMS).

"I started the coalition to give independent record stores a support group to learn from each other," he says, "to make themselves better and stronger, so they could withstand some of this that was going on back then."

CIMS gave birth to other groups, which eventually began Record Store Day, an annual celebration of vinyl and the stores that sell it. Since its first event in 2008, record sales have grown exponentially.

But record stores aren't all Currier has saved. "I was trying to come up with a campaign to champion local business in our community, as national chains and big box retailers were invading our town," he says. "In my head it was about 'Keeping Portland Unique' but that line did not hit a nerve."

During a trip to Austin, he fell in love with the city's "Weird" movement and decided to implement it back home. In 2007, Currier printed 500 bumper stickers, unaware of the impact the simple phrase "Keep Portland Weird" would end up having. What began as a way to support local business has become the unofficial slogan for a city that embraces weirdness.

Address 3158 E Burnside Street, Portland, OR 97214, +1 (503) 231-8926, www.musicmillennium.com, earful@musicmillennium.com | Getting there TriMet to NE Glisan & 32nd (Line 19); free on-site and street parking | Hours Mon–Sat 10am–10pm, Sun 11am–9pm | Tip Cross the river and check out the *Keep Portland Weird* mural (SW 3rd Avenue between W Burnside Street and SW Ankeny Street).

61_Musical Tesla Coil
You've never seen a concert quite like this

Before QuarterWorld opened in 2016, Director of Operations Logan Bowden knew he wanted to feature an attraction that patrons wouldn't expect at an arcade. After traveling the country, he decided he wanted to do something "mad scientist-y" with the space. His first thought was to build a plasma chandelier illuminated by a mini Tesla coil; however, as his research continued, he caught wind of solid state Tesla coils, which possess the ability to produce music. This was what QuarterWorld needed.

Bowden found an engineer based in Chicago who was just eccentric enough for the job, and when the arcade opened, they unveiled Tessi, the only inverted solid state musical Tesla coil in the United States. The contraption measures in at seven feet tall and hangs from the ceiling above a stage in the arcade. It pushes out around 1.3 million volts of electricity and has the ability to throw out 15-foot arcs, though its range is limited by a Faraday cage used to contain the bolts.

Tessi is also unique in the fact that she is equipped with four channels, which means Bowden and his partner Joey Piacentini are able to compose melodic songs using different frequencies and pulse rates to create tones. Their repertoire consists of classical music, movie and television themes, metal, pop, and, of course, video game music. Though four channels are unheard of in a Tesla coil, they're pretty rudimentary in the world of music, so every song composed on Tessi sounds like an 8-bit soundtrack from an old video game – fitting for an arcade.

QuarterWorld hosts 15-minute Tessi shows at 4pm and 9pm every Tuesday and Sunday, with special concerts performed by appointment. The arcade offers free earplugs and protective earmuffs – the noise reaches 90 decibels. But the real spectacle is watching musical lightning wrap around metal with every note. It's truly a hypnotizing sight to behold.

Address 4811 SE Hawthorne Boulevard, Portland, OR 97215, +1 (503) 548-2923, www.quarterworldarcade.com, quarterworld@gmail.com | **Getting there** TriMet to SE Hawthorne & 47th (Line 14); free street parking | **Hours** Tue – Fri 3pm – 1am, Sat & Sun noon – 1am | **Tip** If barcades are your thing, Ground Kontrol on the West Side has been entertaining Portland since 1999 (115 NW 5th Avenue, www.groundkontrol.com).

62 The National Hat Museum

History and hats go hand in hand

When Alyce Cornyn-Selby bought the historic Ladd-Reingold House decades ago, it came with a surprise: Rebecca Reingold's impressive hat collection. As fate would have it, Cornyn-Selby was also an avid collector and decided to showcase the impressive assemblage to the public. In 2005, The National Hat Museum was born.

Though the director passed away in 2017, her apprentice Lu Ann Trotebas inherited the museum and runs tours by appointment only. Those who visit are greeted by the quirky curator, dressed in early 20th-century attire and always donning an extravagant topper. The journey begins in the foyer, as Trotebas reveals the oldest items in the collection: bonnets from the Regency period, dating back to the early 1800s. From there, she whisks you into the Victorian period and then presents the museum's impressive stash of Edwardian hats, the largest collection on public display. Here, she discusses the museum's most impressive pieces: a black 1905 feathered Edwardian in pristine condition, and an *Audubonnet* so rare that the New York historical society copied it in 2018 for an exhibit. She takes you through the 1920s, and subsequent decades – telling history through the eyes of fashionistas and milliners.

Aside from historical context, the museum also houses hats worn by Hedda Hopper, Phyllis Diller, and local icon Darcelle (see ch. 22), as well as set pieces from movies like *Chicago* and *Gangs of New York*. As you ascend to the second floor, the landing pays homage to crowns and Cornyn-Selby's marriage – to her house. Upstairs, Trotebas piques men's interest with an exhibit honoring the evolution of men's hats. There's also a whole room dedicated to Cornyn-Selby's love of silly hats, including the last one she ever made: the "Train of Thought" top hat.

You don't have to be a hat lover to appreciate this eccentric museum, but you may become one after visiting.

Address 1928 SE Ladd Avenue, Portland, OR 97214, +1 (503) 319-0799, www.thehatmuseum.com, info@thehatmuseum.com | Getting there TriMet to SE Ladd & Ladd Circle (Line 10); free street parking | Hours By appointment only | Tip Hat enthusiasts can continue to get their fix by visiting the John Helmer Haberdasher, a family-owned business that was founded nearly 100 years ago (969 SW Broadway, www.johnhelmer.com).

63__Nichaqwli Monument
Critical meeting for the Lewis & Clark expedition

Blue Lake Regional Park is a great place to spend an afternoon swimming, boating, picnicking, hiking, and observing flora and fauna. But long before the disc golf course was plotted and paddle boats were available to rent, this area was a seasonal Chinook fishing village and burial ground. It also served as a critical meeting point between the Lewis & Clark expedition and Native Americans.

In April 1806, William Clark led members of the Corps of Discovery east after spending the winter at Fort Clatsop. The group stopped along the banks of Blue Lake, where they met Nichaqwli (pronounced "nee CHAHK lee") villagers. The explorers had missed the Willamette River in both directions because islands obscured it, so Clark asked a villager to direct him and seven men to the river via canoe. He also hired an elder to draw up a map of the river, tribes, and the number of people in the area, which Clark copied in his journal. This information helped support his prediction that what is now the Portland-Vancouver metropolitan area would be a desirable settlement and port site.

Nichaqwli was also living proof of how smallpox had decimated the region. By the time Clark and his men arrived there was only one functioning lodge in the village, though they saw the remains of five others. They also met a pockmarked woman who survived the disease 30 years prior. By 1830, nearly 90 percent of the population had died.

On Blue Lake's west bank, visitors will find a Nichaqwli Monument that pays tribute to the Chinook tribe in a variety of ways. Red cedar poles with carved faces commemorate the center posts of tribal plankhouses and mythical stories of humans and animals. Carved cedar benches represent canoes, and a basalt net sinker shows the importance of fishing and tool making. On a clear day, the posts and sinker hole each frame a view of Mount Hood, known to Native Americans as Wy'East.

Address 20500 NE Marine Drive, Fairview, OR 97024, +1 (503)665-4995, www.oregonmetro.gov/parks/bluc lake-regional-park, parksandnature@oregonmetro.gov | Getting there On-site parking lot with $5 fee | Hours Daily 8am–7pm | Tip The Lewis & Clark expedition camped at the neighboring Government Island State Recreation Area on November 3, 1805. The island is only accessible by boat and is now part of the Oregon State Park system, with hiking, camping, and fishing (7005 NE Marine Drive, www.oregonstateparks.org).

64 Oaks Bottom Forge
A lesson in blacksmithing

When your GPS says you've arrived at Oaks Bottom Forge, you may be a little confused. You're looking at Alpha Stoneworks, Inc., but where in hell is the forge? You may not be able to see it right away, but you'll probably be able to hear it. Follow the sound of pounding hammers until you see a converted 'K' Line container. You're in the right place.

On any given day of the week, you might see owner Pat Wojciechowski or someone from his team of experienced instructors leading a blacksmithing class. The forge holds six-week sessions year-round, offering everything from Blacksmithing 101 to Bladesmithing. Those interested in taking the introductory course need not have prior experience, and anyone who's completed all of the courses can continue their work through a membership program. A modest one-time fee and monthly payment will get you all the time you want to work in the forge.

In the first course, students learn the fundamentals of blacksmithing – shaping, forming, tapering, flattening, twisting, and punching – and put these skills to work by hammering a traditional wall hook (that's just in the first week). From there, they get to choose two more small projects to complete. These tools usually range from fire pokers to hatchets to railroad spike knives, but Wojciechowski is open to any ideas students may have (he once had someone hammer a frying pan) as long as they focus on moving metal.

Classes meet once a week for three-hour sessions, and the cost of each class includes all your materials. In the spirit of keeping blacksmithing alive, the forge's leadership thinks it's important to make things affordable. If the fee is a bit steep for you, just talk to Wojciechowski, and he'll work something out.

Aside from hosting courses, the forge specializes in building custom knives. Customers can shop online or stop by the forge during retail hours.

Address 2171B SE Moores Street, Milwaukie, OR 97222, +1 (503) 477-7498,
www.oaksbottomforge.com, info@oaksbottomforge.com | Getting there TriMet to
SE Frontage & Ochoco (Lines 34 & 99); free on-site parking | Hours Retail hours
Mon–Sat 9am–5pm; see website for class schedule | Tip You can also find Oak Bottom
Forge knives at the iconic Portland Outdoor Store, along with a wide array of Western wear
and cowboy gear (304 SW 3rd Avenue, www.waterlinkweb.com/portlandoutdoorstore.us).

65 Oaks Bottom Wildlife Refuge

Preserving native flora and fauna

When one of Portland's few remaining wetlands became threatened by industrialization, the city purchased the land to ensure its preservation. Now, those 168 acres of the Willamette River floodplain are Oaks Bottom Wildlife Refuge, a complex of meadows, wetlands, and woodlands that provide a protected habitat to over 175 species of native birds, five species of salamanders, two species of frogs, and a number of fish, including threatened salmon.

The refuge is accessible by trail in Sellwood Park. The sound of chirping birds is cut by the exhilarating screams of adventure seekers at nearby Oaks Park Amusement Park (see ch. 65). But once you get down to the meadow, the path is flat and ideal for an afternoon stroll. Though no bikes are permitted on the trails, the Springwater Corridor that runs parallel to Oaks Bottom makes for a wonderful cycling option. Dogs on leashes are welcome.

The loop trail is a 3.8-mile, family-friendly hike that allows you to observe all that Oaks Bottom has to offer. You'll see butterflies and dragonflies flutter by as you migrate from the meadows to woodlands. Oregon white oak, Pacific madrone, ash, and black locust trees provide a welcome canopy from the beating sun while you make your way towards the wetlands. When the trees begin to thin, you might see great blue herons and other waterfowl swoop down for a snack in the lake. Beavers can be seen busily building dams, while frogs sunbathe on rocks. Hawks, quail, pintails, mallards, and widgeons are just a few other birds that can be spotted in the refuge, making it a spectacular locale for birdwatching.

While marveling at the wildlife around you, it's hard to believe Oaks Bottom is only 10 minutes from downtown Portland. What a perfect urban oasis.

Address SE Sellwood Boulevard & SE 7th Avenue, Portland, OR 97202, +1 (503) 823-7529, www.portlandoregon.gov/parks/finder | Getting there Free on-site parking lot in Sellwood Park | Hours Daily 5am–midnight | Tip In the summer, the nearby Sellwood Riverfront Park is a spectacular way to beat the heat, with an urban, dog-friendly strip of beach to sunbathe before taking a dip in the Willamette River (1221 SE Oaks Park Way, www.portlandoregon.gov/parks/finder).

66 Oaks Park Roller Rink
The last roller rink with a live pipe organ

Oaks Park has been serving the Portland area since May 30, 1905, making it one of the oldest continually running amusement parks in the country. Though always working on new and innovative attractions, the Oaks takes pride in its past and maintains rides until they're no longer able to obtain parts. Because of this, the park houses an eclectic array of attractions ranging from the Herschell-Spillman Noah's Ark Carousel from 1911 and Rock-O-Plane from the late 1940s/early 1950s to the Adrenaline Peak roller coaster, which debuted in 2018. The amusement park operates March through September. However, there's a wonderful piece of history that's open year-round for everyone to enjoy.

The Oaks Park Roller Rink was unveiled in 1906, when the European activity was sweeping America. As visitors skated around the 100×200-foot rotunda floor, the largest in America, an orchestra performed from a platform suspended above the center of the room. In the 1920s, the Oaks invested in its first pipe organ to replace the orchestra. It too floated over the heads of skaters, while an organist played from a separate chamber. In the early 1950s, the park bought its second Wurlitzer, which remains perched upon that aerial structure today. Its current operators, Keith Fortune and Marc Gerlack, perform selections from the *Great American Songbook* every Thursday and Sunday, making Oaks Park the last roller rink in the world to feature a live pipe organ.

If the rink looks familiar upon first visit, you may have seen it in a movie or television show, as it's been featured in everything from *Portlandia* to *Free Willy*. And notice that lane of wavy wood at the back? Those bumps are the result of the Vanport flood (see ch. 108) that destroyed the original floor and caused the Oaks to devise a barrel flotation system under the wood, thus creating the only floating roller rink in the world.

Address 7805 SE Oaks Park Way, Portland, OR 97202, +1 (503) 233-5777, www.oakspark.com, info@oakspark.com | **Getting there** Free on-site parking lot | **Hours** See website for seasonal hours | **Tip** For more historical amusement park fun, head south to the family-owned Enchanted Forest (8462 Enchanted Way SE, Turner, OR 97392, www.enchantedforest.com).

67 __ Old Church Concert Hall
A sanctuary of sound

In 1882, Warren Williams constructed a chapel for Calvary Presbyterian Church on land donated by famed Portland politician and businessman William S. Ladd. The final product is a masterpiece of Carpenter Gothic architecture. High steeples point to the sky and dazzling stained-glass windows beam kaleidoscopic rays of light into the congregation hall when the sun hits them just right.

The church served its original function for nearly a century, before becoming abandoned in 1965. With threats of demolition imminent, a nonprofit organization helmed by local actress and performer Lannie Hurst, who saw the value in saving the beautiful structure, banded together to stave off the wrecking ball. In 1972, the Calvary Presbyterian Church was added to the National Register of Historic Places. It now holds the title of Portland's oldest church building on its original site.

Today, The Old Church (TOC) is a sanctuary of sound rather than sermon. Still run through the nonprofit, the historic building hosts weddings, among other events, but it's primarily used as a concert hall. Because of its residential location, TOC exclusively books stripped down acts, with names like Kishi Bashi and Radiohead's Philip Selway gracing the stage. The Cheshire Cat Lounge, a bar built in the church's old meeting hall, offers patrons libations to sip while listening to the spectacular acoustics bounce off the church's high ceilings, and ogling over the monthly rotating art exhibits that decorate the walls.

Though its purpose is new, its past has been preserved. Everything from the fir pews to the magnificent Hook & Hastings organ are original pieces from the church's first life. There's even a square of the original floral carpeting framed and hanging on display. Those curious to learn more about the church's history need only contact TOC to set up a formal tour.

Address 1422 SW 11th Avenue, Portland, OR 97201, +1 (503) 222-2031, www.theoldchurch.org, staff@theoldchurch.org | Getting there Portland Streetcar to SW 11th & Clay (B Loop & NS Lines); metered street parking | Hours See website for schedule | Tip If historical churches are your thing, head to the nearby First Congregational Church, which was built in 1895 (1126 SW Park Avenue, www.uccportland.org).

68 Oregon Holocaust Memorial

A tribute to victims of a horrific part of history

When Rosa Adler was 20 years old, she and her family were torn from their home in Ulic, Czechoslovakia. The soldiers said they'd be deported and forced to labor in a Russian factory. But when the men in uniform began to squeeze them into cattle cars like sardines, she knew they had lied. Rosa, her mother, brother, and two sisters were sent to Auschwitz-Birkenau, the largest Holocaust killing-center camp. In a year's time, she was victim to Doctor Josef Mengele's horrifying experiments and watched her whole family die. Yet she survived.

As a tour group meets in the Oregon Holocaust Memorial's cobblestone courtyard, scattered with bronzed reminders of the dolls, shoes, and other possessions those affected by the genocide left behind, Peter Wigmore tells Rosa's tragic story. She was his mother. As he talks, the group walks a path crossed with railroad tracks to represent the grueling cattle car trip to hell and arrives at a gravel plaza with a large granite scroll looming.

The first two tablets recount the harrowing tale of the Holocaust, followed by anonymous quotes from survivors plated in bronze surrounded by stone. Peter points out the indents in each plaque. Water fills up behind them and seeps out the cracks, as if the wall is crying. This wasn't intentional, but it's fitting.

On the right end of the scroll lies a boulder and another granite face. Members of the community visited the six camps to retrieve soil and ash. Each bag has been wrapped in a prayer shawl and buried under the rock in a traditional Jewish casket. Along the backside of the wall is an homage to the five million victims who were not Jewish, along with the names of local survivors and their family members who perished in the Holocaust. About halfway through is Rosa Adler Wigmore.

Address 97205 SW Washington Way, Portland, OR 97205, +1 (503) 823-7529, www.ojmche.org/educate/education/holocaust-memorial, info@ojmche.org | Getting there Metered parking in lot | Hours Daily 5am–noon; see website for tours | Tip Continue learning at The Oregon Jewish Museum and Center for Holocaust Education, less than two miles away from the Memorial (724 NW Davis Street, www.ojmche.org).

69__The Oregon Public House
"Have a pint, change the world"

As soon as you step foot into The Oregon Public House (OPH), it's obvious this isn't just another alehouse. The staff are warm and welcoming; children accompany their parents; large groups congregate. It feels like a community, which is fitting considering OPH is the world's first nonprofit pub.

The idea came to Stephen Green, Ryan Saari, and Scott Baker on a hot summer night in 2009. They were sitting in Saari's backyard, lamenting about the recession, when Green made an observation that nonprofits tend to struggle during economic decline. His friends agreed, adding that people also tend to drink more during hard times. That was their lightbulb moment, but it would take nearly four years to make it a reality.

Because they wanted OPH to serve its purpose from day one, the trio was adamant about opening without debt. With the help of hundreds of volunteers, they transformed a century-old building in Portland's Woodlawn neighborhood into a gathering spot for good.

"That's part of the DNA of it," Saari explains, "where we can do something better together."

OPH opened its doors on May 17, 2013, debt-free and ready to spread its "Have a pint, change the world" philosophy. The pub pays its employees industry-standard wages; however, its founders and the rest of the board members work as volunteers to ensure all net profits go to the rotating list of charities OPH partners with each year.

Aside from giving back, it was also important for OPH to serve quality drinks and food – it is an alehouse, after all. They offer a wide range of local beer, including their own Aletruism label, alongside Portland-centric pub food, like sandwiches, burgers, and loads of vegetarian options. Pair that with regular trivia and movie nights, as well as other communal activities, and it's no wonder OPH has been able to raise over $200,000 (and counting) for local charities.

Address 700 NE Dekum Street, Portland, OR 97211, +1 (503) 828-0884,
www.oregonpublichouse.com | **Getting there** TriMet to NE Dekum & 6th (Line 8);
free street parking | **Hours** Mon & Fri 11:30am–9pm, Tue–Thu 4–9pm, Sat & Sun
11:30am–10pm | **Tip** If you're visiting OPH on a Saturday between May and October,
stop by the neighboring Woodlawn Farmers Market at the intersection of NE Dekum
Street and Durham Avenue (www.woodlawnfarmersmarket.org).

70__Oregon Zoo
Rescue Animals
Champions of wildlife conservation and education

The Oregon Zoo is more than just a place to spend the day admiring animals. It strives to educate the community on wildlife respect, conservation, and welfare, as well as environmental literacy. To help achieve its mission, the zoo offers visitor experiences that teach in engaging ways, like an up-close encounter with Josie the Linnaeus' two-toed sloth. During this behind-the-scenes activity, participants are able to feed and take pictures with Josie, and more importantly, learn from her keepers why she was rescued by the zoo and receive a lesson on the dangers of the exotic pet trade.

Though Josie is not viewable to the public, there are over a dozen rescue animals visitors can see on a visit to the zoo. When an animal is found orphaned or injured, it's often sent to a rehabilitation center. After receiving treatment, many of these animals are deemed unreleasable, and that's where the Oregon Zoo comes in. Its staff of trained keepers is able to provide a safe, healthy home to animals that wouldn't survive in the wild. Take for instance Tilly, a river otter that was found wounded near Portland as a pup. With the help of keepers, she not only survived but birthed four pups of her own and acts as a surrogate to the zoo's other orphaned otters. The zoo has also rescued mountain goats, bald eagles, black bears, sea otters, and cougars from locations throughout the Northwest.

There is one rescue animal that made a longer trek, however. The Oregon Zoo is home to Chendra, the only Borneo elephant in North America. She was found in Sabah, Malaysia as a calf – wandering near a palm oil plantation hungry, alone, and scared. She had been shot in the face, which caused blindness in her left eye. The zoo's conservation connection to Sabah is how Chendra found a safe haven and family with Portland's herd.

Address 4001 SW Canyon Road, Portland, OR 97221, +1 (503) 226-1561, www.oregonzoo.org | Getting there MAX to Washington Park (Red & Blue Lines); TriMet to MAX/Oregon Zoo (Line 63); Washington Park Shuttle; metered on-site parking lot | Hours Daily 9:30am–4pm | Tip The Oregon Zoo also has a resident cat named Buddy. He came from the Pixie Project (510 NE Martin Luther King Jr Boulevard, www.pixieproject.org), a nonprofit organization that offers rescue animals for adoption, foster care opportunities, and pet supplies. The Pixie Project sometimes brings adoptable cats to the zoo, so you might end up leaving with a new pet.

71 Original Benson Bubbler

A solution to Portland's drinking problem

On the corner of SW 5th and Washington, a four-bowled bronze drinking fountain continuously gurgles water between the hours of 5:30am and 11:30pm. Towering commercial buildings soar on all sides of the intersection, but there were no banks or hotels guarding over the water fountain when it was built over a century ago. This is the original Benson Bubbler.

As folklore has it, the bubblers originated because local logging tycoon Simon Benson was tired of seeing his millworkers drunk on the job and wanted to give them a non-alcoholic drink to quench their thirst. Others say his inspiration came from seeing a young girl cry on the 4th of July because she couldn't find a drink of water. Either way, the philanthropist donated $10,000 for the purchase and installation of 20 fountains throughout the city.

Today, 52 Benson Bubblers burble fresh drinking water in downtown Portland; however, they do not span past the geographic boundaries the Benson family set in the 1970s in an effort to preserve their uniqueness. In addition to the official four-headed Bubblers, 74 single-bowl variations are scattered throughout the city (there's even a three-bowl fountain near the waterfront), but don't be fooled: these are *not* technically Benson Bubblers. There are a few bubblers that made their way out of downtown, too. In 1965, Portland gifted a fountain to its sister city, Sapporo, Japan. One is also displayed in the Maryhill Museum of Art, and another gifted to Pendleton, Oregon in 2012.

Though the Bubblers are over a century old, the Portland Water Bureau is dedicated to their preservation. The fountains are cleaned bi-weekly and have been improved throughout the years to ensure water conservation. Though they babble continuously nearly 20 hours a day, the Bubblers only use one-tenth of one percent of the city's daily water demand. Doesn't get much more Portland than that.

Address The corner of SW 5th Avenue and Washington Street, Portland, OR 97204 |
Getting there TriMet to SW 5th & Washington (Lines 15 & 51); metered street parking
| Hours Daily 5:30am–11:30pm (barring inclement weather) | Tip Visit Simon Benson's
extravagant Queen Anne-style home on Portland State University's campus (1803 SW Park
Avenue, www.pdx.edu/alumni/simon-benson-house).

72_Outbreak Museum

A tribute to infectious disease outbreaks

Doctor Bill Keene was an eccentric man, known for such quotes as, "Only an idiot would eat raw shellfish," and "Eating cookie dough off the spoon is just as bad as unprotected sex while smoking." But he was as smart as he was outlandish. During his time investigating infectious disease outbreaks for the Oregon Health Department, the epidemiologist was fascinated with preserving recalled products that were implicated in causing an outbreak. When he couldn't find the item (or at least its packaging), he crafted remarkable reproductions.

When he suddenly passed away in 2013, The Northwest Center for Foodborne Outbreak Management, Epidemiology, and Surveillance (FOMES) picked up where he left off. The staff sorted through all of Keene's artifacts (none were labeled, of course), and in 2015 reopened his office as The International Outbreak Museum (IOM), the only one of its kind in the world. Though packed into a small space, the museum holds products from over 150 global outbreaks – and counting. The recalled items range from a box of Rely Tampons, which were associated with Toxic Shock Syndrome and *Staphylococcus aureus* in 1978, to home-jarred beets infected with botulism that ended up killing two people. FOMES is hard at work detecting the cause of outbreaks in the state of Oregon; however, they encourage those interested to send their own artifacts and stories for the museum.

Aside from displaying these vehicles of disease, the IOM is also a tribute to Keene. His relics hang on the walls, including a license plate that says *0157 H7*, the most commonly identified *E. coli* pathogen, alongside photos from his adventures. There's also newspaper clippings and a whole wall of Keene-isms, showcasing some of his best quotes. Because the museum is in the FOMES department of the Portland State Office Building, it's currently open by appointment only.

Address 800 NE Oregon Street, Portland, OR 97232, www.outbreakmuseum.com | Getting there Portland Streetcar to NE Oregon & Grand (A Loop); on-site pay to park lot; metered street parking | Hours See website for tour request information | Tip If science is your thing, OMSI is a wonderful place to let your brain run wild with exhibits ranging from chemistry and physics labs to exploring the USS *Blueback* submarine (1945 SE Water Avenue, www.omsi.edu).

73__Outlaw Grave

Here lies the leader of the Evans-Sontag Gang

While taking a stroll along Mount Calvary Cemetery's rock wall, it's easy to walk right past Christopher Evans' burial site. It's not adorned with a headstone, and when the grass grows out, it obscures some of the engraving. However, the occupant of this unassuming grave had quite the fascinating life.

Best known as the leader of the Evans-Sontag Gang, Evans and his partner John Sontag were infamous for robbing a number of Southern Pacific trains in California during the late 19th century. Their first shootout with the police came on August 5, 1892, in Visalia, California. The outlaws managed to flee to the Sierra Nevada mountains; however, Sontag's brother George was taken into custody. The next day, the duo killed a deputy sheriff, which prompted the largest manhunt in California history. Dozens of lawmen, accompanied by over 300 armed civilians and bounty hunters, scoured the San Joaquin Valley in search of Evans and Sontag, but the outlaws managed to evade capture for 10 months.

On June 11, 1893, the two men were finally cornered at Stone Corral, near Evans' wife's home 10 miles northeast of Visalia. During the shootout Sontag was fatally shot, and Evans was severely wounded – his right arm would later, be amputated. He managed to escape, crawling six miles to a cabin and begging the homesteaders to dress his wounds. A few days later the residents informed police, and Evans was arrested. He was held in Fresno and sentenced to life in Folsom Prison. But he escaped from Fresno County Jail on December 28, 1893. He was caught a month and a half later and served 17 years in Folsom before being paroled in the spring of 1911.

Upon his release, Evans was banished from California and headed north to Portland, where he resided until his death on February 9, 1917, at the age of 69. Though his grave is modest, Evans' story will live on forever in Wild West folklore.

Address 333 SW Skyline Boulevard, Portland, OR 97221, +1 (503) 292-6621,
www.ccpdxor.com | Getting there TriMet to W Burnside & Mount Calvary Cemetery
(Line 20); free on-site parking | Hours Mon–Fri 9am–4pm | Tip While you're there,
ask the office staff to point you in the direction of John Edward Kelly's (better known as
Nonpareil Jack Dempsey) grave. The Irish-born boxer was the first holder of the World
Middleweight Championship in the late 19th century.

74 Paleontology Lab at OMSI

The only hands-on museum prep lab in the US

Anyone who grew up in the Portland area probably took a field trip to the Oregon Museum of Science and Industry (OMSI). Hailing as one of the leading science museums in the country, OMSI has been educating children and adults alike since 1944. Currently housed in a massive, 219,000-square-foot facility, the nonprofit boasts five exhibit halls, hundreds of interactive exhibits, a four-story theater, a planetarium, the USS *Blueback* submarine, and eight laboratories.

As you weave your way through OMSI's various halls, exploring the wonders of space travel, chemistry, and the miracle of birth along the way, you'll see the fossils of a Miomastadon, Sabertooth Cat, and Direwolf while surveying the Earth Science Hall. But what you might miss is the Paleontology Lab, tucked in the back of the hall. The room may look humble, but it's the only traditional museum prep lab in the United States that's also an open exhibit.

Those who decide to enter will find themselves greeted by a friendly coordinator and volunteers eager to share their artifacts. On any given day, curious patrons can examine the skull of an ancient whale with an interestingly placed blowhole and watch staff examine fossils from a roughly 65-million-year-old Triceratops that was dug up in Wyoming. Previous exhibits include the Pacific Northwest residing Sabertooth Salmon and the 228- to 235-million-year-old Thalattosaur, the oldest animal with a backbone found in Oregon.

Children and teens can take their curiosity one step further and participate in the Fabulous Fossils (K–8) and Tools of the Paleontologist (6–12) programs. In these classes, students enjoy a hands-on experience, like helping clean the Triceratops fossils with professional tools, learning to identify different fossils, and creating a 3D copy of a raptor claw to take home.

There are always new things to discover at OMSI if you dig deep enough.

Address 1945 SE Water Avenue, Portland, OR 97214, +1 (503) 797-4000, www.omsi.edu, info@omsi.edu | Getting there MAX to OMSI/SE Water (Orange Line); Portland Street-car to OMSI (A & B Loop Lines); $5 parking in lot | Hours See website for seasonal hours | Tip After all that stimulation, give your brain a break and enjoy a laugh at the nearby Helium Comedy Club (1510 SE 9th Avenue, www.portland.heliumcomedy.com).

75_Peninsula Park Rose Garden

"Stumpton" to "City of Roses"

The International Rose Test Garden is a local landmark. But there's another, older, rose garden in town that's just as beautiful and guaranteed to be less crowded. It is also the site that's responsible for Portland's transition from "Stumpton" to "City of Roses."

The Peninsula Park Rose Garden, designed by parks superintendent and former Olmsted Brothers employee Emanuel T. Mische, was acquired in 1913 as the first home of the Portland Rose Society and Rose Festival Association's official activities. Modeled after classical French rose *parterres*, the sunken rose garden boasts a symmetrical layout centered around a magnificent, decorative fountain with water arcs shooting towards the sky during summer months. In its inaugural year, the garden welcomed 300,000 visitors – more than the city's total population at the time – and was the site where Portland's official rose, the dusty-pink-hued Madame Caroline Testout, was cultivated.

When Washington Park opened in 1917, gears shifted to the International Rose Test Garden, and Peninsula Park fell to the wayside. However, as its centennial loomed, three Oregon State University Master Gardener volunteers with an affinity for the space created a nonprofit called Friends of Peninsula Park Rose Garden in 2012. The group partners with park staff to raise donations and help preserve the oldest public rose garden in Portland and one of only a few formal, turn-of-the-century rose gardens still thriving in the US.

Today, the colorful garden is home to over 5,500 roses representing more than 70 varieties. Though sunken, the rose garden is wheelchair accessible from the north and south entrances. A stroll along the brick paths is a must in early summer, when the flowers are in full bloom. The scent alone is intoxicating. Pair that with Mische's elegant design, and a trip to the Peninsula Park Rose Garden is mesmerizing.

Address 700 N Rosa Parks Way, Portland, OR 97217, +1 (503) 823-2525, www.portlandoregon.gov/parks/finder | Getting there TriMet to N Albina & Ainsworth (Line 4); free street parking | Hours Daily 5am–midnight | Tip After taking a relaxing walk through the rose garden, take time to explore the rest of Peninsula Park, including the playground, splash pad, and historic community center.

76_Pinolo Gelato
Bringing Italian culture to Portland

Sandro Paolini *loves* pine nuts. When he talks about the savory seeds, his eyes twinkle, and a wide grin spreads across his face. He describes cracking the tough shell and collecting the treasure inside – a regular activity during his upbringing in Pisa, Italy, which is known for producing nuts of the stone pine variety – and sprinkling the freshly scavenged seeds on a creamy scoop of gelato. Although that was years ago, his childhood wonder hasn't faded. When Paolini decided to open a business in Portland, he knew he had to incorporate his beloved pine nuts and bring a taste of home to the Pacific Northwest.

On June 21, 2015, Paolini and his partner Ashe Lyon opened Pinolo Gelato on bustling SE Division Street, naming the shop after the Italian word for pine nut. Paolini is staunch about using local milk and fruits, which is why patrons will see flavors rotate with the seasons – peach, melon, and a variety of berries in the spring and summer, and citrus, cranberry, and the fickle quince (which just happens to be another one of Paolini's favorite flavors) in the fall and winter. Interestingly enough, the shop imports hazelnuts from Italy, despite Oregon's reputation as a top hazelnut producer. Paolini thinks those grown in the Pacific Northwest are more suitable for baking than gelato due to their fat content and thick skins.

Although his sweet treats come with a local flare, Paolini's main desire is bringing Italian culture to Portland. His nontraditional flavors are balanced with classics like stracciatella, amaretto, and fior di latte, the Italian equivalent of vanilla and the first flavor Paolini tastes when he visits a new gelateria.

Seeing patrons hang out in the shop for hours, indulging and chatting with friends, brings Paolini immense joy. Especially when they're enjoying a cup of delicately paddled, velvety pine nut gelato.

Address 3707 SE Division Street, Portland, OR 97202, +1 (503) 719-8686, www.pinologelato.com, info@pinologelato.com | Getting there TriMet to SE Division & 36th (Line 2); free street parking | Hours Wed, Thu, & Sun noon–9pm, Fri & Sat noon–10pm | Tip Before (or after) dessert, dine at nearby Ava Gene's, one of the city's best Italian restaurants – and one of the top restaurants in general (3377 SE Division Street, www.avagenes.com).

77__Pips & Bounce

Time travel disguised as ping-pong

Michael and Eugene Jung grew up in Eastern Kentucky, where their primary source of entertainment was a ping-pong table in their family's basement rec room.

"That was our happy place," Michael recalls fondly. But like their youth, ping-pong faded into the depths of memory. In New York City, a group was trying to bring the sport back. The brothers attended an event, and though flooded with nostalgia, they didn't like it's exclusive feel. Ping-pong should be for the masses.

After a year and a half of their own successful pop-up parties in Portland, the Jungs decided to find a permanent home for their ping-pong social club. After draining their life savings and raising money through Kickstarter, Pips & Bounce opened its doors in 2014. With 10 tables, 100 paddles, and 1,000 balls, the club is fun no matter your age. And the best part? You don't have to track down rogue balls.

The interior encapsulates Michael and Eugene's vision: large, white, spherical lights dangle from the ceiling, resembling ping-pong balls. The "play station" is covered in fake oak paneling to replicate the Jungs' basement rec room, vintage posters and all. Walk-ins pay a flat fee for 30 minutes at a table, and reservations and membership packages are available. But Pips & Bounce is so much more than a business.

"What we take delight in is not necessarily how many people come through, but how we've become part of the fabric of life," Michael says. "People make memories here."

They've hosted bar mitzvahs, birthday and retirement parties, anniversaries, and even weddings. With nothing else like it in Portland, a visit to Pips & Bounce is bound to be memorable.

"A customer once said, 'It looks like ping-pong, but you're actually selling time travel'," Michael says. "It takes you back to being 10 years old. It's analog; it's face to face; it's real time. I think, more than anything, we all miss that."

Address 833 SE Belmont Street, Portland, OR 97214, +1 (503) 928-4664, www.pipsandbounce.com, play@pipsandbounce.com | Getting there TriMet to SE Belmont & 9th (Line 15); on-site parking lot; metered street parking | Hours Mon–Thu 3–11pm, Fri & Sat noon–1am, Sun noon–10pm (minors allowed Sun–Thu till 9pm and Fri & Sat till 7pm) | Tip For some more nostalgic fun, head around the corner to Grand Central Restaurant & Bowling Lounge (808 SE Morrison Street, www.thegrandcentralbowl.com).

78__Pittock Mansion

A magnificent feat in technology and architecture

Up a winding road in the West Hills sits a 16,000-square-foot, Renaissance-style château boasting panoramic views of the Cascade Mountain Range, Mount Hood, and the Willamette River. The 46-room estate and 46-acre grounds now belong to the city, but a century ago they were the private residence of Henry and Georgiana Pittock, arguably the most influential figures in Portland history.

Though Henry earned his riches as owner of *The Oregonian* and helped industrialize Portland, he was a modest man with pioneer roots. The Pittocks were more fascinated by state-of-the-art technologies than ornate décor when planning their extravagant abode. The mansion was equipped with innovative lighting and plumbing, a central vacuum system, telephones and intercoms throughout the house, and a dumbwaiter, yet Henry slept in a humble twin bed in his master suite. It was also the first house in Portland with an elevator, which was a selling point for Georgiana who suffered a stroke in 1913, a year before moving in. Today, the historical home museum runs off its original electrical panel and heating supply, and the elevator is still functional.

Aside from tech savvy equipment, the Pittock mansion is also an architectural wonder. As you begin the 23-room tour, you'll notice the house flows in an oval shape around a central marble staircase, like a wheel spoke. The unique design was requested so the Pittocks could enjoy their spectacular views from all living spaces.

Unfortunately, Georgiana and Henry were only able to spend a few short years in their mansion on the hill before passing away in 1918 and 1919, respectively. However, there are those who believe their spirits still live on in their beautiful home. Visitors have reported experiencing a sort of presence during tours, which is generally thought to be Henry, escorting guests like any good host would.

Address 3229 NW Pittock Drive, Portland, OR 97210, +1 (503) 823-3623, www.pittockmansion.org | Getting there Free on-site parking lot | Hours See website for seasonal hours | Tip While exploring the grounds, make sure to step into the Gate House, where groundskeeper James Skene and his wife Marjory lived until the 1940s. The property finally opened to the public in 2018, after years of restoration.

79 __ PlayDate PDX

Where parents enjoy themselves as much as kids do

Bob Birkhahn has five kids, and quite frankly, he grew tired of chasing them around places like Chuck E. Cheese's that are heaven for children and hell for parents. He wanted to go somewhere adults could enjoy too, and when he didn't find that place he created it.

Birkhahn opened PlayDate PDX in 2010 with parents in mind. He laid it out so the indoor playground is confined to one space, with an airy café surrounding it to ensure grown ups can keep an eye on their little ones while getting some rest and relaxation of their own. The café is quiet and softly lit, enabling adults to converse with friends and fellow parents. Its menu boasts handmade pastries and pizza dough, charcuterie boards, and hummus plates, and though the "kid's corner" does offer greasy fare like hot dogs and quesadillas, it also keeps dietary restrictions in mind with items like vegan nuggets and healthy snacks including oranges, baby carrots, and cucumber slices. Best of all? PlayDate PDX is equipped with a full coffee bar for tired parents, and beer and wine for those who really want to unwind.

While adults lounge in the café, kids run wild in the 7,000-square-foot, three-story gym. The structure includes your standard tubes, slides, and netting bridges, but its most popular features are two interactive floors, where kids can choose from a list of rotating games that update monthly, and a ball cannon room, because who doesn't like a foam ball fight? There's also a Toddler Room connected to the gym, where the very young ones can play with foam structures, developmental games, and go down smaller slides. For parents who want to play with their kids, each level is tall enough for them to walk upright.

PlayDate PDX is also affordable. All-day admission for kids 3 and under is very cost-effective, just slightly more for kids 4 and up during the week, and just a bit higher on weekends.

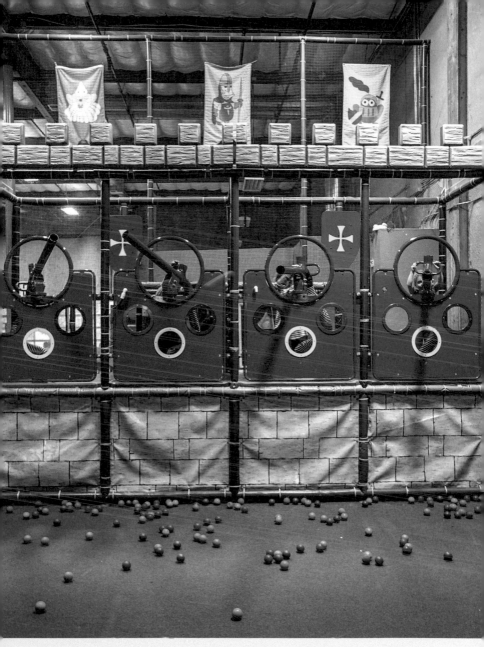

Address 1434 NW 17th Avenue, Portland, OR 97209, +1 (503) 227-7529, www.playdatepdx.com, info@playdatepdx.org | **Getting there** Portland Streetcar to NW 18th & Northrup (NS Line); on-site parking; metered street parking | **Hours** Sun–Thu 9am–8pm, Fri & Sat 9am–9pm | **Tip** For more indoor playground fun visit The Monkey King Play House, which boasts a menu of Chinese-inspired dishes and offers martial arts lessons (17112 SE Powell Boulevard, www.monkeykingplayhouse.com).

80__Poet's Beach
A tribute to the Willamette River

On a hot summer day, there's nothing Portlanders like more than taking a dip in the river. While many people flock to Sauvie Island to wade in the Columbia, Sellwood Riverfront Park to paddleboard in the Willamette, or their favorite swimming hole along the Columbia River Gorge, there's a sandy riverbank much closer to downtown where the water gently laps at the shore.

Poet's Beach is the epitome of an urban beach. Located in South Waterfront, the park is right below the towering Marquam Bridge. During the summer, swim lines and floats calmly bob in the river, delineating a safe place to swim without interfering with boats and other watercraft. The sound of traffic above is oddly tranquil in this setting, with views of the Hawthorne Bridge to the north, Tilikum Crossing (see ch. 105) to the south, OMSI (see ch. 73) to the east, and the city skyline in the distance. But Poet's Beach is more than just a sandy reprieve. It's a tribute to the Willamette River.

Upon arriving at the park, you'll see a sign that explains its purpose: *Engraved into stone along this path are inspired thought from a new generation of children who speak for the Willamette River, and from the Confederated Tribes of Grand Ronde who have honored the river since time immemorial.* As you follow the path down to the sand, take the time to read the powerful words carved in basalt rock lining the way. Chinook words for "eagle," "canoe," "family," and more are etched in stone, along with short poems dedicated to the mighty Willamette written by students ranging from 2nd to 12th grade.

Because it's an urban setting, visitors are encouraged to don footwear both on the sand and in the water. Poet's Beach isn't protected by a lifeguard, so swimmers enter the river at their own risk. But an afternoon of sun, sand, and floating on the water might just inspire you to write some poetry of your own.

Address South Waterfront Park, on the west side of the Willamette River, just north of the I-5 Marquam Bridge, Portland, OR 97201, +1 (503) 823-7529, www.portlandoregon.gov/parks/73880 | Getting there TriMet to Residence Inn-Riverplace (Downtown Express); Portland Streetcar to SW River Parkway & Moody (A Loop, B Loop & NS Lines) | Hours Daily 11am–7pm | Tip The Riverplace Marina is located just north of Poet's Beach and is a wonderful place to take a walk and admire the boats (0315 SW Montgomery Street, www.riverplacemarina.com).

81 Portland Audubon

A wildlife sanctuary just outside downtown Portland

Portland Audubon has been serving the city since 1902. In 1929, the organization purchased its first piece of land, a 12-acre parcel, from a former dairy farm. Today, the nonprofit boasts 172 acres that feature an interpretive center, nature store, administrative buildings, conservation headquarters, hiking trails, and the region's largest and busiest wildlife rehabilitation center.

The Care Center is open 365 days a year and treats roughly 3,000 animals annually, rehabbing everything from baby beavers to baby eagles; injured songbirds to injured skunks. Aside from the wildlife in temporary care, Portland Audubon also houses four educational birds and a turtle that are unreleasable for specific individual reasons. Currently, Aristophanes, a common raven; Bybee, a western painted turtle; Julio, a great horned owl; Ruby, a turkey vulture; and Xena, an American kestrel, all live on-site. Each animal serves as an ambassador for its species and can be viewed in its caged habitat or on the arm of a handler.

Near the educational habitats, visitors can access four miles of trails that cross Balch Creek and wind to a pond swimming with red-legged frogs and rough-skinned newts. On any given day, hikers may spot Steller's jays, American robins, Pacific wrens, pileated woodpeckers, coastal giant salamanders, and other spectacular local wildlife. If you're really lucky, you may see a northern pygmy owl. Just don't bring your four-legged friend on the adventure. Since this is a wildlife sanctuary, no dogs are allowed.

If you're feeling particularly adventurous, you can hike to Portland Audubon from Pittock Mansion (see ch. 77) and check out the Stone House (see ch. 101) on the way. Though the trails and facilities are free to visitors, there are numerous other ways to get involved with Portland Audubon. See the organization's official website for more ideas and information.

Address 5151 NW Cornell Road, Portland, OR 97210, +1 (503) 292-6855, www.audubonportland.org | **Getting there** On-site parking lot; free street parking | **Hours** Interpretive Center/Nature Store: Mon–Sat 10am–5pm, Sun 10am–6pm; trails: daily dawn–dusk | **Tip** Become a part of the Backyard Habitat Certification Program (BHCP), created by Portland Audubon and Columbia Land Trust, and turn your own garden into a wildlife oasis (www.audubonportland.org/get-involved/backyard-habitat-certification-program).

82 Portland Bike Polo
A serious sport without taking itself too seriously

It doesn't matter if it's the peak of summer or the dead of winter – if you visit the Alberta Park tennis court on a Sunday afternoon you're bound to see members of the Portland Bike Polo group playing a pick up game.

Though bike polo historians claim the sport originated in the late 19th century (either in Ireland or India), it wasn't until 1999 that the hardcourt format, which is popular today, started gaining momentum. As legend has it, this version of the game was created by a group of bike messengers in downtown Seattle who wanted to kill time between jobs. They devised courts in alleys, parking lots, and even rooftops. In 2002, a man named Tad Bamford moved to Portland and started his own club in the City of Roses. Since then, the game has spread to roughly 300 cities spanning 30 countries, and governing bodies like North American Hardcourt have formed to create universal guidelines and host tournaments.

Rules differ slightly between clubs, but in Portland they typically play 3v3 style (two teams of three players), and matches last 15 minutes. The game is played with a PVC ball identical to street hockey, a mallet consisting of an UHMW head and aluminum shaft similar to a ski pole, and single-speed bikes specially equipped for polo with a high number of spokes and a front disc brake, among other features. The court is set up with netted goals on each end, and a team scores a point every time a player successfully shoots the ball into the net.

It may be a serious game, but that doesn't mean the players take themselves too seriously. Heckling is a big part of bike polo, as is drinking and building community.

"The best part about bike polo is that it's a group of counterculture freaks who are building their own thing," says club member Jordan Bailey. "We made the rules; we created the spaces that we need; we created the gear. We're all doing it together."

Address 5501–5749 NE 22nd Avenue, Portland, OR 97211, www.portlandbikepolo.org, bikepolo.portland@gmail.com | Getting there TriMet to NE 27th & Killingsworth (Line 17); free street parking | Hours Sun noon–dusk | Tip The nearby Community Cycling Center is a nonprofit organization that celebrates the cycling world by promoting bike safety and selling new and used bikes, parts, and repairs (1700 NE Alberta Street, www.communitycyclingcenter.org).

83 __ Portland Gay Men's Chorus
Championing the LGBTQ+ *community since 1980*

In the spring of 1980, Mark Richards attended a San Francisco Gay Men's Chorus concert and was inspired to start something similar in Portland. He put out an ad in a local gay newspaper, and upon recruiting 20 singers, he founded the Portland Gay Men's Chorus (PGMC) in April 1980, making it the fourth-oldest gay-identified chorus in the country.

Since its inception, PGMC has been a pillar in the LGBTQ+ community. During the AIDS epidemic, the chorus became a beacon of light, growing to more than 100 members. Many of its performances during that time were at the funerals of members, friends, and family, and at the height of the crisis, PGMC had been decimated to less than 30 members. But it persevered.

Today, PGMC boasts over 150 members, and, despite its name, you do not have to be gay nor a man to sing with the chorus. Each year, the organization hosts three "main stage" concerts in Portland: a mission-based performance in March, a Pride pop concert in June, and a holiday show in December, as well as outreach concerts throughout North America. In 2018, PGMC became the first Western LGBTQ+ chorus to tour and perform in the People's Republic of China.

Part of PGMC's mission is to "expand, redefine, and perfect the choral art through eclectic performances," and it takes this to heart with every show, building a repertoire that ranges from classical to blues, Broadway to Motown. With the use of lighting, costumes, and "choralography," no two PGMC concerts are alike.

Most importantly, PGMC's songs aim to champion LGBTQ+ and other underrepresented communities through intentional lyric changes and dance partnerships that eschew hetero- and gender-normative stereotypes. The chorus also produces new commissions that shine a light on the challenges the LGBTQ+ community faces today. Enjoy a concert or even become a member of PGMC yourself.

Address Various locations, +1 (503) 226-2588, www.pdxgmc.org, pgmc@pdxgmc.org |
Getting there See website for performance venues | Hours See website for schedule | Tip If
you'd like to further help the LGBTQ+ community, consider volunteering at Q Center – the
largest LGBTQ+ community center in the Pacific Northwest (4115 N Mississippi Avenue,
www.pdxqcenter.org).

84__Portland Mercado

A celebration of Latinx culture

Portland is admittedly not known for its racial diversity; however, that is slowly changing as more people move to the City of Roses. As a whole, Oregon's Latinx population is increasing at a faster rate than the national average. According to the Oregon Community Foundation, in 2016 the state's Latinx population grew 72 percent since the year 2000, boasting nearly 474,000 residents of Latin American descent. As the number of people rose, so did the amount of Latinx-owned businesses.

Since 2010, Portland nonprofit Hacienda CDC has been hard at work providing developmental help and affordable retail space for Latinx entrepreneurs. Through surveys and extensive research, the organization quickly realized the city's need for a Latinx public market, and in 2015 Portland Mercado opened its doors. Located in the Foster-Powell neighborhood, the market is hard to miss. Colors of vibrant oranges, yellows, greens, and purples catch the eye of passersby, while a row of food carts lure in hungry visitors.

Portland Mercado comprises nine food carts and six indoor vendors, each giving a diverse flavor of Latin American culture. Patrons can munch on everything from Oaxacan mole and Venezualan empanadas to Cubano sandwiches and hefty burritos made to order from the outdoor dining options. Inside, you'll find a meat and produce market, a Nicaraguan coffee shop, a Colombian bakery, a fresh juicery, and a neighborhood bar. Hacienda CDC also champions local Latinx culture with graphics displaying population statistics and a timeline documenting Latinos in Oregon, including the first ever person of Mexican origin to be listed in the Oregon census in 1850.

Aside from the vibrant and enticing retail experience, Portland Mercado also hosts a number of events throughout the year, including farmers markets, live music, and a massive Cinco de Mayo celebration.

Melanie Davis
Owner/Publisher of
El Hispanic News
Portland, Oregon

Address 7238 SE Foster Road, Portland, OR 97206, +1 (971) 200-0581,
www.portlandmercado.org, portlandmercado@haciendacdc.org | **Getting there** TriMet
to SE Foster & 17th (Line 14); on-site parking lot; free street parking | **Hours** Daily
10am–9pm | **Tip** For those yearning to learn Salsa and Bachata dancing, Aztec
Willie's in Northeast Portland hosts highly affordable lessons (1501 NE Broadway,
www.aztecwillies.com).

85 __ The Portland Penny

A simple coin toss can change everything

Portland's name was determined by a simple coin toss. In 1844, Boston, Massachusetts native Asa Lovejoy and Portland, Maine-bred Francis Pettygrove established a land claim on a 640-acre parcel. The site was nicknamed The Clearing or The Village by early residents and passersby canoeing up and down the Willamette River. As Oregon Trail pioneers began arriving in the valley, the developers saw an opportunity to expand their town. Soon, their village was filling with houses, docks, and stores, so Lovejoy and Pettygrove realized their piece of land was becoming a community and needed a name.

During dinner one evening in 1845, the New Englanders decided to let a coin toss determine their town's name. The two were in the parlor of Francis Ermatinger's home in Oregon City when Pettygrove retrieved an 1835 copper penny from his pocket. They agreed to a best two-out-of-three contest. If he won, the site would be named Portland, if Lovejoy won it would be called Boston. Pettygrove called heads, and the rest, as they say, is history.

After spending time in Pettygrove's nephew's safety deposit box in San Francisco following Pettygrove's death in 1887, that fateful penny is now housed in the Oregon Historical Society Museum (OHSM). Those who want to see how Portland got its name need not travel farther than the museum's lobby, where the Portland Penny is displayed. However, you will not regret paying the small admittance fee and viewing its thoughtfully curated exhibits. OHSM's permanent exhibits include the hands-on, kid-friendly History Hub; Oregon Voices, which showcases some of the state's most important people of the modern era; and the dynamic Experience Oregon, which whisks visitors through history, detailing the Native Oregonians, pioneers, and countless other figures who shaped the Beaver State, without shying away from its sordid past.

Address 1200 SW Park Avenue, Portland, OR 97205, +1 (503) 222-1741, www.ohs.org/museum, orhist@ohs.org | Getting there MAX to SW 6th & Morrison (Green & Yellow Lines); TriMet to SW Jefferson & 10th (Lines 6, 38, 45, 55, 58, 68, & 96); metered street parking | Hours Mon – Sat 10am – 5pm, Sun noon – 5pm | Tip Visit the house where the fateful coin toss took place. The Francis Ermatinger House in Oregon City is open for tours on Fridays and Saturdays (619 6th Street, Oregon City, OR 97045, www.orcity.org/parksandrecreation/ermatinger-house).

86__Portland Puppet Museum

The only permanent puppet museum on the west coast

The quaint wood-trimmed building on the corner of SE Umatilla and 9th has been a grocery store, town hall, and a Baptist church in its past lives. Now, it's home to one of only six museums of its kind in the country, and the only permanent one on the West Coast: the Portland Puppet Museum.

Partners Steve Overton and Marty Richmond are lifelong puppeteers and in 2012 decided to make their collection open to the public. Though the puppets are never all displayed at once because they wouldn't all fit in the space, Overton says they own roughly 2,500 puppets that have come from import stores, worldly travels, donations, and the fruits of their own labor. String, hand, rod, shadow, and ventriloquist's puppets are all represented, originating from over 30 different countries. Every four months, the eccentric owners switch out the displays that range from Ancient World, which showcases puppeteering's 4,000-year-old history, to Favorite Fairy Tales, when the storefront is transformed into an enchanted forest – waterfalls, pixies, and all.

The collection features rare puppets, including a set dating back to 1730, as well as 12 original puppets Overton inherited from *Howdy Doody* creator Frank Paris and a Lamb Chop prototype gifted by Shari Lewis, and the Portland Puppet Museum is all about interaction – you won't see any artifacts sitting behind glass cases. They also wanted to make it accessible to all and don't charge an admission fee.

In the summer months, Overton and Richmond's production company, Olde World Puppet Theatre, puts on shows in the courtyard behind the building. The back of the museum, which doubles as a workshop, caters to anyone, children and adults, who wants to play and learn what goes into making one of the extravagant puppets they see on display. You might even get a visit from the Big Bad Wolf, but don't worry – he's a lover, not a fighter.

Address 906 SE Umatilla Street, Portland, OR 97202, +1 (503) 233-7723, www.puppetmuseum.com, news@puppetmuseum.com | **Getting there** TriMet to SE 13th & Umatilla (Line 70); free street parking | **Hours** Thu–Sun 2–8pm; see website for show schedule | **Tip** Awaken your inner child even more at Kidd's Toy Museum. Just be aware that some of the older toys on display may be seen as offensive today (1301 SE Grand Avenue, www.facebook.com/Kidds-Toy-Museum-113578118676868).

87   Portlandia Statue

A copper goddess who's heavily protected

Portlandia towers high above the city, crouched above the entrance of the Portland Building. She's been watching over the City of Roses since 1985, and at 34 feet and 10 inches tall, with a weight of 6.5 tons, she is the second-largest copper repoussé statue in the United States trailing only the Statue of Liberty.

She kneels down, and from the quietness of copper reaches out. We take that stillness into ourselves, and somewhere deep in the earth our breath becomes her city, reads an accompanying plaque by local poet Ronald Talney. *If she could speak this is what she would say: Follow that breath. Home is the journey we make. This is how the world knows where we are.*

The copper goddess is one of the most treasured icons in Portland. So why isn't she publicized?

In 1981, architect Michael Graves was tasked with providing ideas for public art to adorn his newly constructed Portland Building. He proposed using the city's seal as inspiration for a figurative sculpture to greet visitors. The seal depicts an allegorical "Miss Commerce" and several symbols of Portland's agricultural, commercial, and natural resources, including a trident. When sculptor Raymond Kaskey created the statue, he adorned her in the same classical dress as "Miss Commerce" kneeling with the three-pronged spear in her left hand, and her right reaching down to the city.

Though she is public art, Kaskey retains the copyright of *Portlandia*'s image and has heavily protected her from being mass produced. The statue does make a brief appearance in her namesake show's title sequence, though producers have admitted the negotiations with her creator were lengthy.

While it's a shame we don't see *Portlandia*'s image proudly printed on T-shirts, pins, and the like, there's something dignifying about keeping her shrouded from commercial production. It makes viewing her in person that much more breathtaking.

Address 1120 SW 5th Avenue, Portland, OR 97204, +1 (503) 823-4000, www.portlandoregon.gov/OMF/article/587615, cityinfo@portlandoregon.gov | Getting there MAX to City Hall / SW 5th & Jefferson (Orange, Yellow, & Green Lines); metered street parking | Hours Unrestricted | Tip If you want to learn more about *Portlandia*, visit The Standard's exhibit dedicated to the statue across the street from where she stands, on the second floor lobby of the Standard Plaza Building (1100 SW 6th Avenue).

88_ReBuilding Center

Building a better Portland

The ReBuilding Center (RBC) began in a Boise neighborhood garage in 1997 as a way to give back to the community. Now, the nonprofit takes up nearly a city block of North Mississippi Avenue. Since its humble beginnings, the organization has strived to divert reusable products from the waste stream and make resources more accessible by selling recycled building materials at up to 90 percent off market value.

The sprawling open-air warehouse is hard to miss for passersby. Its entrance is adorned by a grove of ornate community trees made of cob and a kaleidoscopic stained-glass window. Upon entering, you're greeted by an old piano ready to be played, the resident cat, Ella, and a sea of used household products ranging from stovetops to cabinet doors. Items obtained by donation and deconstruction are organized by type, with each section named something quirky like Tub Town Turnpike and Appliance Alley. Across from the warehouse looms a massive lumber yard offering a variety of wood planks for ambitious DIYers. For those worried that their purchase won't work when they install it at home, fear not – a team of staffers and volunteers assure each piece is in working order before it goes on the floor.

Aside from the eight tons of materials moving through the warehouse each day, RBC also houses an expansive woodshop that offers hands-on classes covering everything from women's DIY carpentry to plumbing repairs and electrical education. The sessions are offered both to the public and as private team-building or employee training courses.

Though RBC is a DIY haven, you don't have to be crafty to want to pay it a visit. The 50,000-square-foot space is decorated with vibrant murals and donated artwork, making for an eye-catching exploration experience. Even the cash register mirrors RBC's message with an engraved wooden sign stating, *EVERYONE WELCOME.*

Address 3625 N Mississippi Avenue, Portland, OR 97227, +1 (503) 331-9291, www.rebuildingcenter.org, info@rebuildingcenter.org | **Getting there** TriMet to N Mississippi & Beech (Line 4); free street parking | **Hours** Mon–Sat 10am–6pm, Sun 10am–5pm | **Tip** After purchasing household wares, head to the nearby Pistils Nursery for botanical goods (3811 N Mississippi Avenue, Suite 1, www.pistilsnursery.com).

89 __ Rhododendron Garden

A botanical oasis in Southeast Portland

Crystal Springs Rhododendron Garden is a relaxing escape from city life, and some of its botanical inhabitants have called the land home for over 100 years. The oldest rhododendron in the current garden was planted prior to 1917, when famous Portlander William S. Ladd owned the property. By the mid-20th century the land became neglected and overgrown, but with help from the Portland Chapter of the American Rhododendron Society, the garden began to flourish and hosted its first rhododendron show in 1956. In 1964, it was officially named the Crystal Springs Rhododendron Garden.

Today, the 9.5-acre botanical oasis houses more than 2,500 rhododendron, azalea, and companion plants, many of which are rare or hybrid breeds you wouldn't normally see in the Pacific Northwest. The surrounding Crystal Springs Lake also attracts nearly 100 species of birds and waterfowl – as well as the occasional beaver and nutria – making it a tranquil setting for birdwatchers. You may even see a coveted bald eagle.

While the garden's annual foliage and water features, which include babbling springs, fountains, and small waterfalls, make it a year-round destination, the ideal time to visit is late April to early May, when the rhododendrons are in peak bloom. Bursts of yellows, pinks, purples, and reds stretch as far as the eye can see, while ducklings attentively follow their mothers in the lake and nearby paths. If you're able to stay for sunset, you won't be disappointed. The view is stunning as the sun sinks beneath Portland's West Hills, painting the sky vibrant colors reminiscent of the garden's magnificent blooms.

The park is open year-round from dawn until dusk. Between March 1 and September 30 there is a nominal admission fee from 10am to 6pm, Wednesdays through Sundays. At all other times, admission is free – and it's always free for children under the age of 12.

Address 5801 SE 28th Avenue, Portland, OR 97202, +1 (503) 771-8386,
www.portlandoregon.gov/parks/finder | Getting there TriMet to SE Woodstock & 32nd
(Line 19); free street parking | Hours Daily Apr 1–Sep 30 6am–10pm; daily Oct 1–Mar 31
6am–6pm | Tip Golf enthusiasts can play a round at the neighboring Eastmoreland Golf
Course (2425 SE Bybee Boulevard, www.eastmorelandgolfcourse.com).

90 Rimsky-Korsakoffee House
An old "haunt" with a jaw-dropping bathroom

Rimksy-Korsakoffee House was slinging bowls of cappuccino before it was cool. The nondescript Craftsman house is shrouded in foliage and displays no signage (it never has and never will); however, despite the intentional lack of marketing, Goody Cable has managed to keep her business alive and well since 1980, making it one of the oldest coffee shops in Portland.

Once you find the elusive pink house and walk inside, it's like you've been transported into an alternate version of the past. To the left of the foyer is a creaky staircase, and to the right is the parlor. On any given night, a classical musician could be playing the in-house grand piano (the place is named after Russian composer Nikolai Rimsky-Korsakov, after all), while patrons order drinks and decadent desserts from "haunted" tables that have a tendency to rotate, grow, and vibrate unexpectedly. Knickknacks line the walls and a hodge-podge of light fixtures hang from the ceiling.

Though the atmosphere downstairs is delightfully creepy, it's what's upstairs that is truly remarkable. Once your coffee or tea has run through you, make it a point to take a potty break. The unisex bathroom is located up the old, wooden staircase. When you arrive on the second floor, you'll see a series of doors. *Not Here* the first one cautions; the second has no doorknob at all; the third quips *NOT HERE, SILLY!* The fourth warns *DON'T EVEN THINK ABOUT COMING IN HERE!* Through a process of elimination, you'll find the right door, and when you open it you're transported once again – under the sea. Without giving too much away, let's just say there are fish and mermaids all around, and an interesting pair of feet splash off a dock above your head.

Rimsky's is a whimsical, spooky part of Old Portland lore. Just be sure to bring cash (it's all they accept) and prepare to stay up late, as it doesn't open until 7pm.

Address 707 SE 12th Avenue, Portland, OR 97214, +1 (503) 232-2640 | Getting there
TriMet to SE Belmont & 11th (Line 15); on-site parking lot; free street parking | Hours
Sun–Thu 7pm–midnight, Fri & Sat 7pm–1am | Tip Also check out the neighboring Pied
Cow Coffeehouse, an equally fascinating café/bar housed in an old Victorian with
a sprawling patio that doubles as a hookah garden (3244 SE Belmont Street).

91 River View Cemetery

The final resting place of prestigious Portlanders

When Portland pioneers Henry Corbett, William S. Ladd, and Henry Failing purchased 350 acres of land in the southwest hills, it was for one reason: establishing an inclusive, nonprofit cemetery. They opened River View in 1882, and the name was fitting – the expansive land boasted panoramic views of the Willamette River and Cascade Mountain Range. However, the founding fathers strived to make the grounds just as scenic as the backdrop and planted their own arboretum of Douglas fir, cedar, Japanese maple, magnolia, and chestnut trees, among others. In the century that's passed, those saplings have grown to towering heights, becoming homes for resident bald eagles and confining the sights beyond to specific vista points.

Though now shrouded in tree cover, the cemetery is still a magnificent place to take an afternoon walk and pay a visit to some of Portland's most prominent people. Corbett, Ladd, and Failing have all been laid to rest in Founder's Square, near the cemetery entrance. The influential Pittocks (see ch. 77) are right across the path, next to local suffragette hero Abigail Scott Duniway (see ch. 110). Up the winding hill, you'll find beer pioneer Henry Weinhard's monument, O.K. Corral leader Virgil Earp, professional football player Lyle Alzado, and infamous Major League Baseball pitcher Carl Mays, known for being the only player to throw a fatal pitch. Among the many strong women buried at River View are Lola Baldwin, the country's first female police officer, and Hazel Ying Lee Louie, one of the first Chinese-American women to earn a pilot's license and fly for the United States military.

With so much history on its grounds, River View Cemetery offers a variety of walking tours via its online app, and through paper brochures. Just pop into the office upon your arrival to pick up the information that best suits your interests.

Address 0300 SW Taylors Ferry Road, Portland, OR 97219, +1 (503) 246-4251, www.riverviewcemetery.org | Getting there TriMet to SW Taylors Ferry & Riverview (Line 43); on-site parking lot | Hours Mon–Fri 8:30am–5pm, Sat 9am–5pm, Sun 11am–4pm | Tip Just across the Sellwood Bridge, you can feast your eyes on the quaint, mid-19th-century Oaks Pioneer Church that was moved three times before rooting in its current location (455 SE Spokane Street, www.oakspioneerchurch.org).

92__Roosevelt's Terrariums
Plant a miniature rainforest in a whiskey bottle

When Gregg "Roosevelt" Harris first opened his terrarium shop in 2015, profit was not his concern. In fact, he was prepared to diminish his savings slowly to keep it open. He had been planting terrariums for nearly 50 years at that point and wanted to teach his teenage son James the arts of botany and business. It was a passion project.

Now, the father-and-son-run store is not only thriving, but it's the most popular place in the country for terrarium planting classes. Gregg and James offer six to eight classes per week, teaching students the history, science, design, and maintenance of a true, self-contained terrarium. Customers pay a reasonable fee, plus the cost of materials, and are able to customize their container, soil, gravel, charcoal, moss, and plants. Once they take their terrariums home, Roosevelt's offers a no-fault warranty: if anything fails to thrive, they take responsibility and will repair or replant when need be. Lucky for them, only one in 50 of their terrariums fail. They also trim, clean, and water terrariums for tips, kind of like a terrarium spa.

"The shop has been an amazing vehicle for me to design the kind of life I want to live," says Gregg, who not only looks up to the shop's namesake but also seconds as a Theodore Roosevelt imper-sonator for educational performances. Aside from the name, the store's aesthetic mirrors that of Roosevelt's time with Mission Oak furniture and taxidermy décor, and classical music coming through the speakers.

Those interested in pre-planted terrariums have plenty to choose from in the store gallery, from old whiskey bottles to traditional Wardian cases. Some even come with poison dart frogs, though Gregg stopped selling them separately. "I didn't start this busi-ness to work hard," he says with a laugh. "I want to putz around. I enjoy the social aspect, planting, and teaching, but I want to keep it simple."

Address 1510 SE 44th Avenue, Unit 101, Portland, OR 97215, +1 (503) 734-9996, www.rooseveltspdx.com, rooseveltspdx@gmail.com | **Getting there** TriMet to SE Hawthorne & 44th (Line 14); free street parking | **Hours** Tue–Fri noon–5pm, Sat 11am–6pm | **Tip** If you're in search of a poison dart frog (or other creature) for your terrarium, Gregg suggests Tropical Hut (4106 SE Division Street, www.thetropicalhut.com) and Pets on Broadway (2762 NE Broadway Street, petsonbroadway.com).

93__Rose City Rollers

The largest roller derby league in the world

While most patrons visit Oaks Park to get their adrenaline pumping on thrill rides or try their luck with carnival games, there's another group that congregates at the amusement park for a totally different reason. Near the back of the property resides The Hangar, and on any given evening it's packed to the rafters with hundreds of fans cheering on their favorite roller derby team.

Since the Rose City Rollers were founded in 2004, it's become the largest roller derby league in the world, boasting over 600 female-identifying skaters that range in age from 7 to their late 50s. The league is divided into Junior and Adult teams and offers opportunities for every skill set from recreational to the world championship-winning all-star travel team, Wheels of Justice. However, it's the home teams that lace up the most in The Hangar.

Every season, the Break Neck Betties, High Rollers, Heartless Heathers, and Guns N Rollers vie to become adult home team champion. The teams play each other twice throughout the year, and conclude with a double-header championship in the spring to determine the top three teams.

The energy during these bouts is electric. The bleachers are full of fans and past players sporting gear to support their favorite teams. Cheers echo throughout the spacious building as the fearless jammers muscle their way past tough blockers to score points for their team. Though it's clear who's cheering for whom, you won't hear trash talking at a game – above all else, the Rollers strive to create a welcoming, inclusive environment.

During the summer, the Rollers provide orientations for those interested in joining the league, as well as camps and rec games. In the fall, home teams host away teams to fundraise for the following season. They host nearly 40 events annually, so you're bound to find a way to support the Rollers no matter the time of year.

Address SE Oaks Park Way, Portland, OR 97202, www.rosecityrollers.com,
info@rosecityrollers.com | Getting there Free on-site parking lot | Hours Refer to the Rose
City Rollers' website for event information | Tip Though food and drink are available to
purchase at a Rose City Rollers event, the nearby Muddy Rudder Public House is a great
place to hang out after a bout (8105 SE 7th Avenue, www.muddyrudderpdx.com).

94__Rosetown Ramblers
Portland's LGBTQ+ *square dance club*

On the second Saturday of every month between September and June, the Oak Grove Community Club transforms into a honky tonk as the Rosetown Ramblers host their monthly social square dance. Some guests wear traditional getups of Western shirts, cowboy boots or billowing square dance skirts, while others dress casually. Members often sport Ramblers gear, like vests with the group's boot and rose emblem or T-shirts that spell out its slogan "These colors don't run, they sashay" underneath a large rainbow flag. You see, the Rosetown Ramblers aren't your average square dancers. They're Portland's LGBTQ+ club, and they have been since the early 1980s.

When the Ramblers were founded, it was in response to bars' unwelcoming attitude toward the LGBTQ+ community. Fortunately, the times have changed, and honky tonks are (for the most part) accepting; however, there's still something to be said for gay square dance clubs. For one, they welcome *everyone*. Secondly, they're not as sedated and heteronormative as more conventional dance halls. You won't find dress codes here, and while dances are sometimes led by traditional callers, they incorporate "fluffs," or little fluctuations that you wouldn't see at a straight dance. Simply put, gay square dance clubs just have more fun.

But that doesn't mean they don't take square dancing seriously. During a typical social, dancers are expected to retain around 68 calls. The two-hour-long events alternate between Mainstream and Plus level Modern Western Square Dance calls that are packaged into two-song tips, usually split between pattern and singing calls. The only requirement to attend a dance is, well, knowing how to square dance. Luckily, Rosetown Ramblers also offer lessons that run from January to May or September to December. For a reasonable fee, you can immerse yourself in a 16-week program that will get you dancing with the best of them.

Address 14496 SE Cedar Avenue, Portland, OR 97267, +1 (503) 610-8154, www.rosetownramblers.com, info@rosetownramblers.com | **Getting there** TriMet to SE 34th & Maple (Line 34); on-site parking lot; free street parking | **Hours** See website for social dance and lesson schedules | **Tip** For more country-and-western fun, spend an evening at the Landmark Saloon (4847 SE Division Street, www.landmarksaloon.com) listening to live music and drinking whiskey, or whatever your drink of choice may be.

95 __ Sauvie Island Spaceship
Washed up boat turned graffitied curiosity

Crossing over the Sauvie Island Bridge from industrial Northwest Portland is like entering a new world filled with quiet agriculture and relaxing riverside beaches, so it's no wonder a UFO landed there. Er, sort of.

Collins Beach, on the east end of the island, is full of surprises. Aside from it being clothing-optional, it's also the site of the Sauvie Island Spaceship. The structure is tucked away in the trees, but you can easily spot it from the sand, thanks to its colorful, graffitied exterior. Its spherical shape and small, circular windows make it look like a flying saucer, but where did it come from and how did it end up on the island's shore?

Sorry *X-Files* enthusiasts, but the vehicle isn't from a far away planet. Its origin is Hubbard, Oregon. A civil engineer by the name of Richard Ensign built the 31-foot, concrete paddlewheel boat in the early 1970s for the purpose of being able to make a fast getaway should society collapse. In 1973, it was towed to a dock on the Willamette River and made its maiden voyage. Ensign, along with a crew of eight, sailed to the coastal town of Astoria. The two-sailed trimaran, nicknamed the Floating Saucer, could sleep 12 people and was equipped with a wood stove. The ship was in use on and off for two decades, until the Willamette Valley flood of 1996 swept it away and washed it aground on Collins Beach. Though it's too high to get inside without assistance, visitors have thoughtfully propped up logs and engineered a climbing rope for anyone who wants to access the boat's hull.

Those curious to find the Sauvie Island Spaceship need just arrive at the second or third Collins Beach parking area and make the short trek through the brush towards the water. The Floating Saucer is situated in-between the two markers. But don't be shocked if you see more than the graffitied shipwreck once you arrive at the nude beach.

Address NW Reeder Road, +1 (503) 823-7529 | **Getting there** Permit parking along the road near the Collins Beach entrance | **Hours** Daily 4am–10pm | **Tip** If Collins Beach's lax clothing rules make you feel uncomfortable, there are plenty of other beaches on the island where you can wade in the Columbia River with other swimsuit-clad visitors (www.traveloregon.com/places-to-go/cities/sauvie-island).

96 Shanghai Tunnels
Time travel to Portland's dubious years

Portland was established as a port town in the mid-19th century. As its population grew, so did business. A series of tunnels snaking to Willamette River docks were built underneath Chinatown for legitimate reasons, such as keeping supplies dry and away from traffic. However, criminals known as crimps also conducted business in Portland's Underground, running opium dens and brothels, and kidnapping, or "shanghaiing," people for blood money.

Though some claim shanghaiing is a myth, the Cascade Geological Society (CGS) is a group of historians who've done tremendous amounts of research about Portland's past. CGS hosts a number of Shanghai Tunnels tours that touch on everything from ghost stories to ethnic history, but the general structure is the same.

Groups meet at Hobo's restaurant and are briefed on a short history of the city before descending underground. Equipped with flashlights, a tour guide takes you along a cleared out portion of the tunnels while explaining Portland's place in shanghaiing lore. As the story goes, kidnappings took place between 1850 and 1941 with an estimated 3,000 people being captured at its peak. Able-bodied men were drugged with a combination of ether and opium mixed in their drink and dropped from a trap door built into the tavern floor. From there, they were locked in claustrophobic cells, drugged again, and dragged to the docks, where they were sold to ship captains. Women were advised not to travel alone for fear of being taken and sold into underground prostitution. Though police were aware of the crimps' sordid practices, they kept their mouths shut with bribes or fear of being kidnapped themselves.

During the tour you'll see uncovered artifacts ranging from opium dens to holding cells, concluding in a Shanghai Tunnels museum filled with items collected from the tunnels. This local history lesson isn't just for tourists.

Address Tour groups meet at Hobo's restaurant (120 NW 3rd Avenue, Portland, OR 97209), +1 (503) 622-4798, www.portlandtunnels.com, www.shanghaitunnels@onemain.com | **Getting there** MAX to Old Town/Chinatown (Red & Blue Lines); TriMet to W Burnside & NW 2nd (Lines 12, 19, & 20); metered street parking | **Hours** See website for tour information | **Tip** After the tour ends, head over to Old Town Pizza & Brewing for dinner. You might just be seated next to its resident ghost, Nina, a victim of Portland's vile underground (226 NW Davis Street, www.oldtownpizz.com).

97__She Bop
A sex shop catering to every body

When you first walk past She Bop, you might not think anything of it. The signage resembles that of a quaint boutique. And it is. Sort of.

Upon closer examination, you'll realize you can't see inside the windows. Read the sign a little closer and notice the store's mantra: "A female-friendly sex toy boutique for every body." When co-founders Evy Cowan and Jeneen Doumitt opened She Bop's doors in November 2009, it was with this particular mission in mind.

"Our goal was to take the taboo out of shopping for sex toys," Cowan explains. "We wanted coming into She Bop to feel like coming into any other specialty boutique: light, bright, comfortable, friendly, educational, and fun! We wanted to promote exploration and empowerment."

Through the help of a friendly, knowledgeable staff, She Bop has become a safe haven for even the most timid customers. First time buying a dildo? No problem. Curious in exploring anal play? Wonderful! The person behind the counter will help you find the items that most fit your needs and make you feel comfortable in the process. You also don't have to worry about the quality of the products here – Cowan and Doumitt are selective about what stocks their shelves. Everything they carry is body-safe and non-toxic.

"Through conversation and exploration, we can often help determine what might work for each individual, and folks tend to leave much more comfortable talking about sex toys then they were when they came in. We love that!" Cowan gushes. "My favorite is when people walk out the door and I can hear them 'woohooing' right after they leave the shop. Priceless."

Aside from retail, She Bop also offers monthly educational classes that tackle topics ranging from oral sex workshops to reconnecting with your sexuality after trauma. The original store is in the Mississippi neighborhood, with a second location on SE Division Street.

Address 909 N Beech Street, Suite A, Portland, OR 97227, +1 (503) 473-8018, www.sheboptheshop.com, info@sheboptheshop.com | Getting there TriMet to N Missi-ssippi & Beech (Line 4); free street parking | Hours Sun–Thu 11am–7pm, Fri & Sat 11am–8pm | Tip Cross the river to the West Side and support more badass women at the feminist clothing boutique, Wildfang (404 SW 10th Avenue, www.wildfang.com).

98__ The Simpsons' Portland

How Matt Groening's hometown inspired his art

When Matt Groening named his fictitious town Springfield, it was intentional. He realized the name was one of the most common in the United States, and he wanted it to resonate with fans no matter where they lived. But let's be real – *The Simpsons* is based on its creator's hometown of Portland.

In the show, the Simpsons live on Evergreen Terrace, which also happens to be the street Groening grew up on with his mom Margaret, dad Homer, brother Mark, and sisters Lisa, Maggie, and Patty. Aside from personal influences, the cartoonist also pays homage to the city by naming most of his characters after local roads. NE Flanders Street reminds you of the Simpsons' "okily dokily" neighbor Ned (vandals have slapped a "D" on the street sign several times). It's not surprising that villainous "Sideshow" Bob Terwilliger was named after the treacherous Terwilliger curves, and Milhouse's last name Van Houten comes from an avenue in North Portland. Meanwhile, Montgomery Burns' name is a nod to two historic (read: old) Portland locales, Montgomery Park and Burnside Street. Take a stroll through the Alphabet District, and you can walk past the namesakes of Reverend Lovejoy (NW Lovejoy Street), Mayor Quimby (NW Quimby Street), and even schoolyard bully Kearney Zzyzwicz (NW Kearney Street).

The Portland native has admitted to getting bullied for being bookish and getting in trouble for drawing in class but still must have love for his alma mater, Lincoln High School, because he gave another artist permission to give it a permanent gift. Fellow cartoonist Matt Wuerker etched Bart Simpson – signature spiky hair, T-shirt, shorts and all – into wet cement and wrote "Class of 1972" in the iconic *Simpsons* scrawl, commemorating Groening's graduation year. The art is on public display, located along SW 18th Street just south of Salmon.

Address Various locations | Getting there Varies by location | Hours Unrestricted | Tip
Drive a few miles up into the West Hills, and you can find the house where Groening grew
up with the real Homer, Marge, Lisa, and Maggie (742 SW Evergreen Terrace).

99__Stag PDX

A gay strip club, and so much more

When its doors first opened in 2015, Stag was known for being the second all-nude gay strip club on the West Coast. (Fun fact: the first is Silverado, which also calls Portland home.) But since its current owner Michael Francis got the keys to the bar, it's become so much more than a male strip club.

Sure, you'll still see guys bare it all while swinging on a pole, but the club's programming has branched out to offer events that cater to just about everyone. There's amateur night, body positivity night, lesbian night, and drag queen-emceed dance nights spinning everything from EDM to hip-hop. In early 2019, Stag also became one of the only venues in the country to host trans strip nights that champion all stages of transition. Dancers from near and far have traveled to the City of Roses to participate in the club's femme and masc events, including famed trans porn star Viktor Belmont, and Aydian Dowling, the first masc trans model to be on the cover of *Men's Health*.

"It's all about bringing everyone together," Francis says. "I just want everyone to get along and have a good time."

Though Stag's technically a gay bar, its main goal is to provide a safe space for the whole LGBTQ+ community. But it doesn't stop there. Francis wants it to be a truly inclusive place where anyone can feel comfortable and let loose (he likes to equate the atmosphere to *Cheers*). As such, it allows bachelorette parties (as long as they don't distract the dancers) and puts on a Drag Brunch every Sunday, hosted by a rotating list of iconic Portland drag performers.

"On the weekends when I see the room's filled with straight people, gay people, trans people, lesbian people, I love it," Francis gushes. "I hope it shows that everybody can be in one room together and not judge each other, not hate anybody, and that everybody just loves each other. Ultimately, that's the goal."

Address 317 NW Broadway, Portland, OR 97209, +1 (971) 407-3132, www.stagpdx.com, info@stag-pdx.com | **Getting there** TriMet to NW Broadway & Davis (Line 17); MAX to NW 6th & Davis (Green & Yellow Lines); metered street parking | **Hours** Mon & Tue 7pm–2am, Wed–Sat 5pm–2am, Sun 11–2am | **Tip** Silverado, the first all-nude gay strip club on the West Coast, is just down the street from Stag (610 NW Couch Street, wwww.silveradopdx.com).

100__ Star Theater

The place to thank for Portland's strip club scene

Portland is famous for having more strip clubs per capita than any other city in the United States, and the Star Theater's former owner, John Tidyman, is one of the reasons why.

The venue has had many lives since opening its doors in 1911. What began as a silent film house turned into a burlesque club that starred the famous Tempest Storm before becoming an adult movie theater. In the 1970s, the city sued Tidyman for violating an obscenity statute after obtaining one of the controversial flicks the Star screened during live sex and strip shows. To Portland's surprise, the Oregon Supreme Court ruled in the businessman's favor in 1988, stating his theater's activities were protected under Article 1, Section 8 of the Oregon Constitution: "No law shall be passed restraining the free expression of opinion, or restricting the right to speak, write, or print freely on any subject whatever."

The very next year, the first all-nude strip club opened in the City of Roses. Today, Portland boasts the second most strip clubs in the country, behind only Houston – a city with quadruple the population.

Since the historic *City of Portland vs. Tidyman* ruling, the Star has exchanged hands several more times. Film director Gus Van Sant owned it for several years. It's been a restaurant. It's been a nightclub. Now, under the ownership of Frank Faillace, the Star has been reborn again as a music and performance venue.

Upon purchasing the property in 2011, the local entrepreneur celebrated its 100th birthday by rebuilding a replica of the original marquee. Inside, newspaper clippings and old burlesque posters tell the Star's colorful history. Storm even performed a one-night show in 2013.

Though commemorating its past, the theater's newest iteration mainly books live music events, hosting big names ranging from Alt-J to Dick Dale.

Address 13 NW 6th Avenue, Portland, OR 97209, +1 (866) 777-8932,
www.startheaterportland.com, dantesstartheater@gmail.com | **Getting there** TriMet to
SW 6th & Burnside (Lines 8 & 9); MAX to SW 6th & Pine (Green & Yellow Lines);
metered parking | **Hours** See website for schedule | **Tip** If you want some devilish fun, check
out Faillace's other club Dante's, which is a quick walk from the Star (350 W Burnside
Street, www.danteslive.com).

101__Stone House

A comfort station with a discomforting past

At the junction of the Wildwood and Lower Macleay trails in Forest Park rests an old stone ruin covered in moss and graffiti. The building once had windows and a roof, but those are long gone. Set next to a babbling creek, a passerby may think this stone house was once the dwelling of a reclusive artist or thoughtful writer, but no. It was a comfort station (i.e. restroom) that served hikers from its construction in 1929 to its decommission in 1962, after the infamous Columbus Day Storm damaged its water supply system beyond repair. The Park Bureau dismantled the structure to its skeletal form. In the decades that passed, it became one with its lush, green surroundings. Forgotten.

In the 1980s, the stone house was resurrected when local high schoolers stumbled upon its remains on the trail and sanctioned the sturdy foundation as a party site, fondly naming it The Witch's Castle. Though the ruins bear no connection to sorcery, in fact, the land on which they reside is haunted by a sordid past.

In the mid-1800s, Danford Balch moved to Portland from the East Coast and settled on a donation land claim of roughly 346 acres, including the site of the Stone House, with his wife Mary Jane and their nine children. Danford quarreled with the neighboring Stump family, and after his eldest daughter Anna eloped with Mortimer Stump against her father's wishes, he became unconsolable. Danford killed Mortimer with a shotgun in front of witnesses on the deck of the Stark Street Ferry. After evading police and hiding out in the woodsy part of his land, Danford was captured in July of 1859. A month later, he was tried and convicted of murder.

On October 17, Danford was hanged in front of 500 onlookers, marking the first legal hanging in the city. The creek on the trail bears his name because people still referred to the land as the Old Balch Place for years after his death.

Address Wildwood Trail, Portland, OR 97210, +1 (503) 823-7529, www.portlandoregon.gov/parks/finder | Getting there Park at the Upper Macleay parking lot and follow the Wildwood Trail for half a mile | Hours Daily 5am–10pm | Tip Just across the street from the Upper Macleay parking lot is the lovely Adams Community Garden, which was donated to the city by Nina B. Adams in 1968 (4300 NW Cornell Road, www.portlandoregon.gov/parks/finder).

102__Sunlan Lighting
Get lit

Even if you've never been inside Sunlan Lighting, chances are you're familiar with the store – or at least its exterior. The shop is known for its intricate window settings, ranging from politically charged displays on the importance of inclusiveness to complex lego scenes. But the front window shows passersby what to expect behind the door: any type of lightbulb you could ever imagine.

"How can I light up your life?" Kay Newell asks every customer who walks through her door. It's a question she's been asking the Mississippi community for decades, always with a smile on her face.

When the businesswoman first opened up shop, she strived to help illuminate a neighborhood that she describes as the most dangerous in Portland. These days, it's one of the most hip and happening quadrants of the city, but Newell's mindset is the same. She likes to find light in the dark and spark joy in each person who visits her store through puns, hand-drawn cartoons, quirky aesthetic, and above all else, great customer service.

If you ask Newell, she'll tell you her lightbulb shop is the only one of its kind in the country. Her labyrinthine store offers everything from incandescent Edison bulbs to the most modern LEDs, and everything in-between. She sells holiday lights, full-spectrum sunshine lights to combat Seasonal Affected Disorder, and much more. She also sells wiring and tools for DIYers and commercial fixtures for the less handy.

"You're changing my mind about lighting right now," a first-time customer declared earnestly after listening to her tutorial on different types of LED bulbs. Newell smiled and encouraged him to come back and play sometime. To her, the best salesperson is honest and sincere. Running a successful business for over 30 years in a neighborhood that has gone through an intense period of gentrification is testament to that philosophy.

Address 3901 N Mississippi Avenue, Portland, OR 97227, +1 (503) 281-0453, www.sunlanlighting.com, kay@sunlanlighting.com | **Getting there** TriMet to N Mississippi & Failing (Line 4); free street parking | **Hours** Mon – Fri 8am – 5:30pm, Sat 10am – 5pm | **Tip** Paxton Gate offers another quirky shopping experience just up the street from Sunlan, geared more toward those who like things like fossils, taxidermy, framed insects, and other oddities (4204 N Mississippi Avenue, www.paxtongate.com).

103 __ Tattoo 34 on Hawthorne

A minority-run tattoo shop that emanates good vibes

Portland is a hub in the tattoo world, but you'd be hard pressed to find a shop quite like Tattoo 34 on Hawthorne in the City of Roses. Tattoo artist Toby Linwood and his wife Nisha Supahan purchased what used to be Hawthorne Ink in 2016 and transformed it into one of the few (if not only) minority-run tattoo parlors in the city. Toby is of African-American, Native American, and First Nations descent, and Nisha is Native American and Scottish. Together, they strive to create an environment that is inclusive to all walks of life. And it's working.

Aside from the impeccable work their team provides to customers, the biggest compliment Toby and Nisha receive is the good vibes their shop emanates. Though there are plenty of top-notch artists to choose from in Portland, regulars find themselves attracted to Tattoo 34 because of its sense of community. The staff regularly chat with each other during sessions, and Toby admits that many of his clients become personal friends after he works on them.

"It's a small space, so we're constantly telling jokes, giving each other a hard time. People are laughing a lot," Toby says with a smile. "People will come in, and they'll have amazing tattoos from other places, but all they can associate them with is a bad experience with the tattoo artist. It takes away from the quality of work, and we don't want that to happen here."

When asked, Toby will say he specializes in fine-line black and gray work and lettering, but according to Nisha, he can do everything. Toby's only requirement is that he gets to draw the design you choose for your tattoo – he doesn't feel comfortable tracing over someone else's design.

Though walk-ins are welcome, anyone who wants work done by Toby is recommended to book an appointment in advance. And don't worry about bringing cash, Tattoo 34 is a rare parlor that accepts credit cards.

Address 3401 SE Hawthorne Boulevard, Portland, OR 97214, +1 (503) 235-3606, www.tattoo34pdx.com, info@tattoo34pdx.com | **Getting there** TriMet to SE Hawthorne & 34th (Line 14); free street parking | **Hours** Daily noon–8pm and by appointment | **Tip** Bison Coffeehouse is another Native American owned establishment that is making strides in Portland (3941 NE Cully Boulevard).

104_ TIGL

A barber shop focused on community

You feel the love in The Influential Grooming Lounge (TIGL) from the second you walk in. Barbers and hairdressers welcome you with a smile and enthusiastic greeting before getting back to engaging conversations with clients. It's a bubbling, uplifting atmosphere, and co-owner Art Williams wouldn't have it any other way.

"I've always believed that the barbershop is the community. It's the place you go to learn about any and everything," he explains. "If you want to know what's going on in the community, go talk to the folks in the shop. You'll get all the answers you're looking for."

Williams knew he wanted to be a barber at the age of 15. As he worked his way through college and got a job at his dream company, he always cut hair on the side. It was a passion he couldn't shake. Eventually, he accepted his true calling and enrolled in barber school. Since 2003, Williams has been cutting hair professionally, working in and running shops up and down NE Martin Luther King Jr Boulevard.

In 2017, the entrepreneur was ready for a new challenge and couldn't pass up the opportunity to purchase a shop with his partners Jayson Jean Baptiste and Harold Fowlkes. Since its opening, TIGL has been a pillar for the neighborhood. Aside from providing impeccable service and building relationships with clients, the shop also focuses on giving back to the community. It partners with a number of local churches and nonprofits to help with everything from collecting food and clothing for the homeless to offering blood pressure checks and healthcare education to clients.

"It's not just TIGL partnering to give back – the people do as well. When they bring in food for Thanksgiving dinners and toys for Christmas, it's a collective effort and the community loves it," Williams says. "We genuinely care for every person that gets a service in our shop."

Address 3262 NE Martin Luther King Jr Boulevard, Portland, OR 97212, +1 (503) 444-7928, www.theinfluentialgl.com, theinfluentialgl@gmail.com | Getting there TriMet to NE Martin Luther King Jr & Fargo (Line 6); street parking | Hours Tue–Sat 10am–7pm | Tip Want to get your haircut by a former NBA player? Check out Terrell Brandon's Barber Shop (1330 NE Alberta Street).

105 — Tilikum Crossing Lights
Aesthetically pleasing, scientifically intriguing

If you live in or have visited Portland since 2015, chances are you've walked (or biked, or taken mass transit) across Tilikum Crossing, Bridge of the People. It was a big deal upon completion, as it's the city's first new bridge to cross the Willamette River since 1973 and the first major bridge in the US designed for pedestrian, transit, and cyclist traffic only. Without the distraction of private cars, a trip across Tilikum Crossing serves as a peaceful time to reflect. But if you live in or have visited Portland since 2015, you probably already knew that. You also probably already know that the bridge is lit in alternating colors every night. But what you might not know is how and why the shimmering lights shine the way they do.

There are 178 LED lights strategically placed along the bridge's 40 cables, four transmission towers, and above and below the deck. The lights were designed by installation artists Anna Valentina Murch and Doug Hollis, and digital artist Morgan Barnard developed a program that translates data from the river itself into an aesthetic display. When the Willamette's water is temperate, the lights project warm colors like orange and yellow. When the temperature's frigid, cooler greens and blues illuminate the bridge.

Tide also affects the lights. When it comes in, the colors move toward the middle of the bridge. When it goes out, they move to the ends. Tide levels also determine the speed of the lights: at high and low tide, they move faster, and they go at a slower pace at midpoint. The river's speed dictates how swiftly the colors change: the faster the currents, the quicker the colors cycle through. Lastly, the river height affects contrast in the lights. When the water is higher the colors are more contrasted and change in movement and pattern. You may view the bridge in a different light the next time you view it at night.

Address South of the Marquam Bridge and North of the Ross Island Bridge, Portland, OR 97201, www.trimet.org/tilikum | **Getting there** MAX to South Waterfront/SW Moody (Orange Line); TriMet to South Waterfront/SW Moody (Lines 9, 17, & 291) if coming from the west side; MAX to OMSI/SE Water (Orange Line), TriMet to OMSI/SE Water (Lines 9 & 17) coming from the east side; limited parking on either side of the bridge | **Hours** Unrestricted | **Tip** While on the east side of the bridge, enjoy a bite and a beer in a converted train car at Mt. Hood Brewing Co. Tilikum Station (401 SE Caruthers Street, www.mthoodbrewing.com).

106 _ Troll Bridge

You must pay the troll toll

In Nordic mythology and Scandinavian folklore, trolls have been terrorizing humans for ages. Generally described as monsters with deformed bodies, claws, fangs, and, on occasion, multiple heads, trolls were known to lurk in caves, on mountains, and under bridges, waiting to pounce on an unsuspecting victim. Many who encountered the nefarious beasts could outwit them – trolls aren't known for their smarts. Yet it was never a pleasant experience to stumble upon one. But in 1959, the world of trolls changed forever.

Danish woodcutter Thomas Dam couldn't afford to buy his daughter a Christmas gift, so he carved a troll from his imagination. The gift was a hit among children in their town, and Dam's company began producing plastic dolls under the name Good Luck Trolls. These are the wide-eyed, bejeweled bellied, wacky-haired trolls Americans know and love, and these are the creatures you'll meet when you visit the Troll Bridge.

If you wind your way along NW McNamee Road on the outskirts of Portland, you'll come across an old trestle railroad bridge. There, nailed to the weathered planks, are dozens of troll dolls in various shapes and sizes. Some are characters from the *Trolls* film series; some are the colorful dolls Dam made popular; some are painted directly onto the wood, and some are downright creepy. While the bridge's residents are mainly innocuous, there were a few visitors who decided to pay the troll toll in headless dolls (or sometimes *just* the head), or eerily adorned toys.

When you arrive at the Troll Bridge, do be aware that you have to stand in the middle of the street to admire the art. Parking can also be tricky, as the streets are narrow and don't provide much of a shoulder. Aside from the funky spectacle, the bridge is in a truly breathtaking locale, surrounded by lush forest and woodlands that are worth a visit all of their own.

Address 16498 NW McNamee Road, Portland, OR 97231 | Getting there Free street parking at your own discretion | Hours Unrestricted | Tip If you're visiting the bridge in the fall, make a stop at The Pumpkin Patch on Sauvie Island to enjoy hayrides, corn mazes, barnyard animals, autumnal treats, and, of course, picking pumpkins (16511 NW Gillihan Road, www.thepumpkinpatch.com).

107 __ UP Soccer Superstars

Where Megan Rapinoe got her start

Anyone who's been to a University of Portland (UP) Pilots soccer game at Merlo Field has seen some of its most prestigious players standing larger than life above the seats. Before Megan Rapinoe was making headlines during the US women's soccer team's memorable and inspiring 2019 World Cup run, she was making waves at her alma mater. During her freshman season in 2005, the midfielder/winger helped lead the Pilots to an undefeated season that resulted in their second national championship. That same year, Christine Sinclair celebrated her senior season by notching a second NCAA title on her belt – the star forward was also on the Pilots team that took home the school's first championship in 2002.

In the years that followed their historic collegiate careers, Rapinoe has gone on to win a gold medal in the 2012 Olympics and two World Cups in 2015 and 2019, while Sinclair has represented her native country of Canada in five World Cups and took home bronze medals in the 2012 and 2016 Olympic Games.

Both women have become legends on the UP campus and are memorialized with those banners showcasing their professional achievements draped throughout the Merlo Field grandstand, where the Pilots play their home games. The neighboring Chiles Center houses trophy cases commemorating the school's national championships and showcasing jerseys from their most memorable alumni. Aside from Rapinoe and Sinclair, UP has also cultivated professional soccer talents like Sophie Schmidt, Stephanie Lopez, Shannon Mac-Millon, Tiffeny Milbrett, Elli Reed, Keelin Winters, and men's soccer players including Conor Casey, Nate Jaqua, Kasey Keller, Steve Cherundolo, Heath Pearce, and Luis Robles.

In addition to soccer, UP also runs quite an impressive sports program for women and men. Tickets are available to Pilots sporting events throughout the year.

Address 5000 N Willamette Boulevard, Portland, OR 97203, +1 (503) 943-7117,
www.portlandpilots.com | Getting there TriMet to N Willamette & University of Portland
(Line 44); free on-site parking lot | Hours See website events schedule | Tip You can see
Christine Sinclair play on Portland's professional women's soccer team, the Thorns FC, who
play at Providence Park (1844 SW Morrison Street, www.timbers.com/thornsfc).

108_Vanport

A housing project that changed Oregon's demographic

Oregon is known historically for its lack of racial diversity. Due to discriminatory laws, less than 2,000 of Portland's 360,000 residents were Black before World War II. But during wartime, everything changed.

Within a year of the US entering World War II, more than 160,000 people moved to Portland to work in home front industries, which attracted African Americans from the South. By 1941, the city was a major shipbuilding center, but there wasn't enough housing for the influx of workers. Oregon Shipbuilding Corporation's owner Henry Kaiser took matters into his own hands and purchased 648 acres of low-lying farmland situated between Portland and Vancouver to build a temporary housing complex. Construction took 110 days, and at the end of 1942, residents started moving into the slipshod buildings. Vanport quickly became the largest housing project in the US and the second-largest city in Oregon. At its peak, approximately 6,000 of the 40,000-plus residents were Black, and Vanport is heralded for hiring the state's first Black teachers and police officers.

Between 1940 and 1950, Portland's Black population increased more than any other West Coast city besides San Francisco and Oakland; however, segregation was still apparent. There was only one other housing project that accepted African Americans. After the war, many Black families stayed in Vanport, having nowhere else to go.

At 4:17pm on May 30, 1948, a portion of the dike surrounding Vanport broke, and within minutes the city was destroyed. Only 15 people lost their lives in the flood, but 18,500 were displaced, roughly 6,300 of which were Black. Many Black families stayed in Portland, however, forever changing the city's ethnic demographic.

All that's left of Vanport is a plaque standing in an open field, but the imprint it left on Portland is an integral part of the city's checkered history and one that won't be forgotten.

OREGON HISTORY

Vanport
Oregon History

Within a year of the US entering World War II, more than 160,000 people moved to Portland—a city of only 360,000—to work in Home Front industries. Industrialist Henry Kaiser's three shipyards employed the most workers. To house his employees and their families, Kaiser persuaded the US Maritime Commission in 1942 to fund the nation's largest public housing project. Within 10 months, Kaiser had built an entire community on 640 acres of low-lying farmland—Vanport.

The First of Its Kind

Vanport soon became Oregon's second largest city, nicknamed Kaiserville. Most Vanporters lived in one-bedroom apartments. There was a library, post office, police station, infirmary, public cafeteria, stores, and a 750-seat movie theater. While most Americans had no medical issues once, Kaiser's workers enjoyed a prepaid health plan. After the war, the plan and its doctors became the Kaiser Permanente medical and dental care program.

Henry Kaiser highlighted above.

A groundbreaking 24-hour daycare program, the largest in the world, cared for preschoolers and older children and cooked hot take-home meals for parents returning from the shipyards.

School classes and faculty for Vanport's 6,000 children were racially integrated. Schools ran seven days a week in two shifts.

Swept Away

In 1948 at 4:17 p.m. on Memorial Day, a portion of the dike surrounding Vanport was broken. The Columbia River, swollen with early spring snowmelt, flowed quickly into Vanport. Floodwaters fifteen feet deep washed Vanport away.

Residents had been assured by authorities that the dikes were holding and that they would be warned in ample time to evacuate. The break caught everyone, including the authorities, by surprise. Thankfully, sloughs within Vanport absorbed the initial surge, allowing approximately 40 minutes for most people to flee Vanport to higher ground along Denver Avenue. Still, 16 people lost their lives in the flood.

With an overwhelming number of displaced people, private citizens took many Vanporters into their homes. Bitterness over the lack of proper warning by the authorities resulted in a civil case; however, the courts decided the federal government could not be held responsible for a natural disaster.

Dikes surrounding Vanport presumably would protect it from flooding, but an old railroad cut that had been filled in as part of the dike on the western side of Vanport was too easily gave way.

After the war, pioneering aspects of Vanport's child and health care programs remained popular examples of what a private enterprise and the government could achieve when united in a common purpose—an experiment in the full utilization of life.

Sponsored by: **KAISER PERMANENTE.**

Address 2579–2593 W Delta Park, Portland, OR 97217 | Getting there MAX to Delta Park/Vanport (Blue & Yellow Lines); free parking | Hours Unrestricted | Tip Support local business and the Black community by grabbing a cup of joe at Deadstock Coffee Roasters (408 NW Couch Street, Suite 408, www.deadstock.com).

109__ The Wishing Tree

This tree sprouts more than leaves

There's a tree in Northeast Portland that sprouts more than leaves – an elm that towers outside Nicole Morantz Helprin's Irvington neighborhood home, decorated in hundreds of manila tags. Though the sight may be peculiar to those unaware, this is the Wishing Tree, and it's become a whimsical staple in the community.

Helprin transformed the elm after becoming inspired by her friend's wishing tree in San Francisco. In 2013, when her children complained of boredom, she suggested they create a wishing tree of their own. Together, they sought out nails, pens, and manila tags, and constructed a sign instructing passersby to write a wish on the tag and hang it on a nail hammered in the tree. In the years that have passed, the tree has become a destination of sorts and proudly wears the wishes and dreams from people all over the world. But in fact, some of Helprin's favorite messages were written during the project's infancy.

"When we first started the tree, my daughter Lola was just starting kindergarten," she recalls. "We invited her entire class to write and illustrate wishes and hang them on the tree. Those remain some of my favorites. Kids wished for their siblings to be nicer to them. There were wishes to be ninjas, teleporters, and mermaids. And wishes for happiness and prosperity for their parents. They thought big and with their hearts."

Though she recognizes there are trees like hers all over the world – wishes are universal after all – Helprin thinks there's something different about the words left on her elm. "The wishes on this tree feel special," she says. "Many are wishes for strangers or the world. Others are wishes for other people or the neighborhood."

It's also become a place of solace for those grieving. "People come to gather to wish for their sick children, or to remember a lost loved one," Helprin says. "There's no right way to wish."

Address 2954 NE 7th Avenue, Portland, OR 97212 | Getting there TriMet to NE M L King & Morris (Line 6); free street parking | Hours Unrestricted | Tip If you stop by the Wishing Tree on a sunny day, pack a picnic and spend the afternoon at nearby Irving Park (707 NE Fremont Street, www.portlandoregon.gov/parks/finder).

110__Woodlark Hotel
Suffragette City

In 1908, the French Renaissance-style Cornelius Hotel first opened its doors. Known as The House of Welcome, Dr. Charles W. Cornelius' 66-room hotel was desired for its proximity to Portland's luxurious shopping and theater districts. It also housed the Ladies Reception Hall, a regular meeting place for local suffragists.

Abigail Scott Duniway led the charge in Oregon's fight for gender equality. The outspoken, often controversial activist celebrated the victory of woman suffrage in the Idaho territory in 1896 and the state of Washington in 1910, after her early successes were overturned; however, it took more of a fight to win women the right to vote in Oregon, where she resided her whole adult life. Oregon defeated women's suffrage more times than any other state, and Duniway endured five losses – in 1884, 1900, 1906, 1908, and 1910 – before women were finally able to vote in 1912. She also displayed activism through her writing. Duniway edited and published a human rights newspaper in Portland called *The New Northwest* for 16 years (1871–87), as well as journals, weeklies, and 22 novels that addressed women's rights, including 1859's *Captain Gray's Company*, which was the first commercially published novel in Oregon.

Duniway's 40-year role in women's suffrage granted her the titles of Oregon's "Mother of Equal Suffrage" and "Pioneer Woman Suffragist of the Great Northwest."Her legacy lives on at the Woodlark Hotel, which fuses the historic Cornelius Hotel and Woodlark building and restored the Ladies Reception Hall – original tiling, paint color, and all – into a floral-walled, plush-seated bar called Abigail Hall. Patrons can nosh on old-fashioned menu items like prawn cocktails and Waldorf salads, and sip reimagined versions of classic cocktails, while discovering the many suffragist Easter eggs strewn throughout the blush and teal colored room.

Address 813 SW Alder Street, Portland, OR 97205, +1 (503) 548-2559, www.woodlarkhotel.com, info@woodlarkhotel.com | **Getting there** Portland Streetcar to SW 10th & Alder (A Loop & NS Lines); TriMet to SW Washington & 9th (Lines 15 & 51); metered street parking | **Hours** Abigail Hall: daily 3pm–midnight | **Tip** Abigail Scott Duniway passed away in 1915, just before her 81st birthday. Her final Portland residence was at the Fordham Apartments (742 SW Vista Avenue).

111 The Zymoglyphic Museum

The intersection of art and nature

Through the door of a Mount Tabor garage awaits the Zymoglyphic Museum, a self-described "Fictocryptic Portland Institution."

As patrons reach the top of the steps, they're welcomed by collections of Jim Stewart's self-made artifacts, neatly organized by the fabricated Zymoglyphic region's key time periods. Relics line the shelves, and dioramas fill fish tanks like a miniature natural history museum documenting fictitious scenes. Taxidermy is mixed with flora and found objects to create a fantastical world that blurs the line between nature and art.

Though the museum's current incarnation opened in 2016, Stewart has been fascinated with nature since the age of 10, cataloging rocks, arrowheads, marine animals, bird's nests, and fossils. Interested in science and anthropology, he began to experiment with building his own artifacts in the 1970s. After acquiring an old clock face and brass base, Stewart decided to put the two together, along with some cogs, a doll's arm, and a crab claw. He called it the Self-Destroying Automaton and devised a wondrous backstory for his creation and the time period from which it came, aptly named The Age of Wonder.

"This particular mechanical wonder was a clockwork automaton that not only told time but continuously removed pieces of itself and offered them to passersby," he wrote of the piece. "How the internal parts were regenerated has yet to be determined despite intensive investigation by the museum staff."

Without knowing it at the time, Stewart had pieced together the first of what would become over 200 handmade relics on display in his awe-inspiring museum. Now retired, the former software engineer is constantly working on new art, using a mix of found, donated, and purchased material.

Address 6225 SE Alder Street, Portland, OR 97215, www.zymoglyphic.org, zymoglyphic@gmail.com | Getting there TriMet to SE Belmont & 62nd (Line 15); free street parking | Hours First and fourth Sundays of every month 11am–4pm | Tip Before letting your imagination wander at the museum, grab a pint at the nearby Caldera Public House (6031 SE Stark Street, www.facebook.com/calderapublichouse).

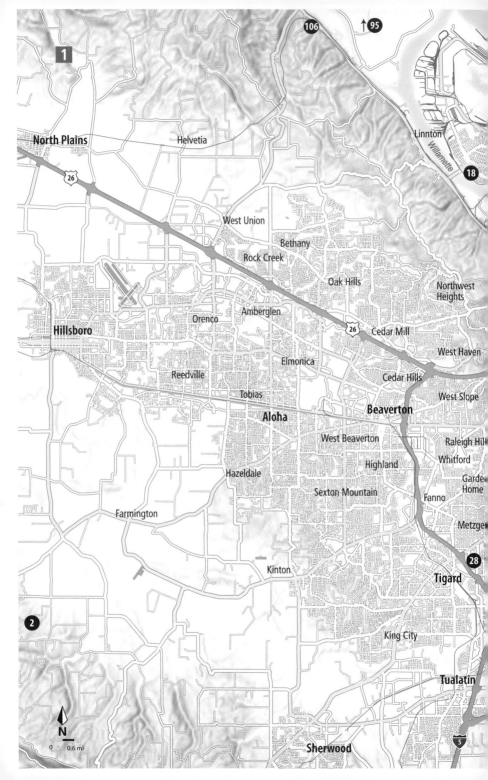

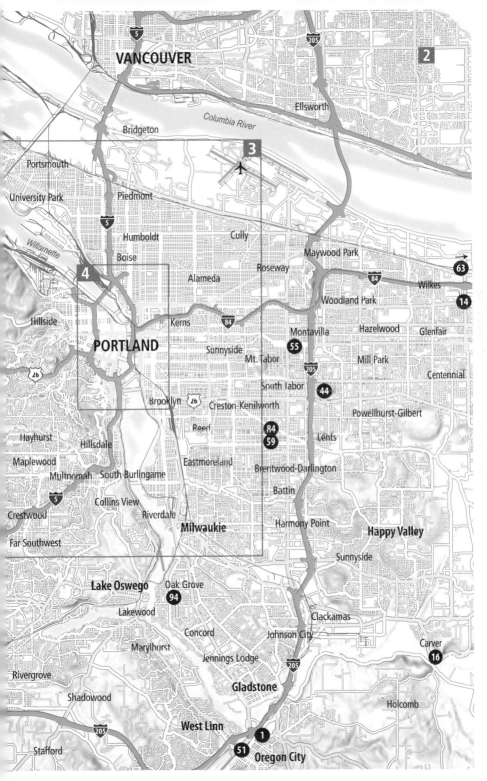

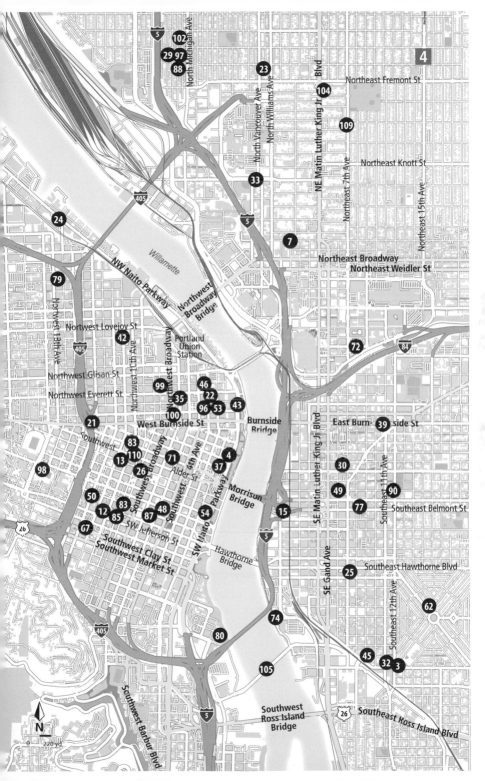

Dave Doroghy, Graeme Menzies
111 Places in Vancouver
That You Must Not Miss
ISBN 978-3-7408-0494-7

Kelsey Roslin, Nick Yeager
111 Places in Austin
That You Must Not Miss
ISBN 978-3-7408-0748-1

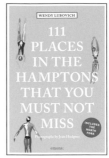

Wendy Lubovich, Jean Hodgens
111 Places in the Hamptons
That You Must Not Miss
ISBN 978-3-7408-0751-1

Sandra Gurvis
111 Places in Columbus
That You Must Not Miss
ISBN 978-3-7408-0600-2

Michelle Madden, Janet McMillan
111 Places in Milwaukee
That You Must Not Miss
ISBN 978-3-7408-0491-6

Floriana Petersen
111 Places in Silicon Valley
That You Must Not Miss
ISBN 978-3-7408-0493-0

Joe Conzo, Kevin C. Fitzpatrick
111 Places in the Bronx
That You Must Not Miss
ISBN 978-3-7408-0492-3

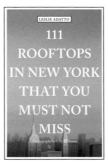

Leslie Adatto, Clay Williams
111 Rooftops in New York
That You Must Not Miss
ISBN 978-3-7408-0495-4

John Major, Ed Lefkowicz
111 Places in Brooklyn
That You Must Not Miss
ISBN 978-3-7408-0380-3

Wendy Lubovich, Ed Lefkowicz
111 Museums in New York
That You Must Not Miss
ISBN 978-3-7408-0379-7

Anita Mai Genua, Clare Davenport,
Elizabeth Lenell Davies
111 Places in Toronto
That You Must Not Miss
ISBN 978-3-7408-0257-8

Benjamin Haas, Leonie Friedrich
111 Places in Buenos Aires
That You Must Not Miss
ISBN 978-3-7408-0260-8

Andréa Seiger
111 Places in Washington
That You Must Not Miss
ISBN 978-3-7408-0258-5

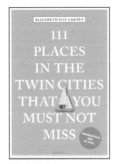

Elisabeth Larsen
111 Places in The Twin Cities
That You Must Not Miss
ISBN 978-3-7408-0029-1

Joe DiStefano, Clay Williams
111 Places in Queens
That You Must Not Miss
ISBN 978-3-7408-0020-8

Allison Robicelli, John Dean
111 Places in Baltimore
That You Must Not Miss
ISBN 978-3-7408-0158-8

Amy Bizzarri, Susie Inverso
111 Places in Chicago
That You Must Not Miss
ISBN 978-3-7408-0156-4

Laurel Moglen, Julia Posey,
Lyudmila Zotova
111 Places in Los Angeles
That You Must Not Miss
ISBN 978-3-95451-884-5

Gordon Streisand
**111 Places in Miami and the
Keys That You Must Not Miss**
ISBN 978-3-95451-644-5

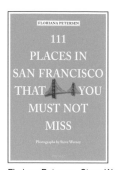

Floriana Petersen, Steve Werney
**111 Places in San Francisco
That You Must Not Miss**
ISBN 978-3-95451-609-4

Jo-Anne Elikann
**111 Places in New York
That You Must Not Miss**
ISBN 978-3-95451-052-8

Frauke Kraas, Regine Spohner,
Jörg Stadelbauer
**111 Places in Myanmar
That You Shouldn't Miss**
ISBN 978-3-7408-0714-6

Christoph Hein, Sabine Hein
**111 Places in Singapore
That You Shouldn't Miss**
ISBN 978-3-7408-0382-7

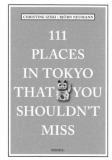

Christine Izeki, Björn Neumann
**111 Places in Tokyo
That You Shouldn't Miss**
ISBN 978-3-7408-0024-6

Kathrin Bielfeldt,
Raymond Wong, Jürgen Bürger
**111 Places in Hong Kong
That You Shouldn't Miss**
ISBN 978-3-95451-936-1

John Sykes, Birgit Weber
**111 Places in London
That You Shouldn't Miss**
ISBN 978-3-95451-346-8

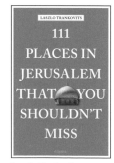

Laszlo Trankovits
**111 Places in Jerusalem
That You Shouldn't Miss**
ISBN 978-3-7408-0320-9

First and foremost, thank you to the Emons team for trusting me with telling Portland's story – I literally would not have been able to do this without you – and special thanks to my editor Karen Seiger, who was always there to bounce ideas off of while always trusting my judgement, ensuring this list was the best it could be. To my talented photographer Jason Quigley, thank you for bringing each chapter to life with your impeccable work. It was such a pleasure taking this journey with you, and even more so creating a friendship that I know will last long after the book is published. To my friends who were always excited to help me explore the nooks and crannies of our wonderful city, and to my husband Nathan for his unconditional support throughout this whole process – you kept me sane. To the countless people I interviewed, thank you for your grace, your humor, your knowledge, and your trust in me to tell your tales. Portland's stories are your stories, and I'm beyond grateful to share them with the world.
K. N.

Thank you most of all to my wife, Megan. This project was a huge logistical challenge, and you were supportive the whole way despite my absurd, unpredictable schedule. You were also full of ideas, suggestions, and calm vibes when things got overwhelming. Thanks to my daughters Charlotte and Lila for making me a better person, and for your willingness to pose and make silly faces if I need to test a lighting idea. To my parents, thank you for always being there for me. And to Katrina, thank you for being such a joy to work with and for keeping us on track to finish this project on time. You have vividly and succinctly described an amazing variety of places, and I'm honored to have my photos accompanying your excellent writing. Thanks to the Emons team and our editor Karen Seiger for giving us so much creative freedom throughout the course of our work. Finally, thank you to all the people who let us into your establishments, shared your talents and passions, and posed for photographs.
J. Q.

Katrina Nattress has been writing professionally since 2008, but her love for local culture began far before then. Born and raised in the Portland area, Katrina has always been fascinated with exploring the nooks and crannies of her city. There are still hidden treasures that have stayed under the radar despite the city's rapid growth. These are the places she holds dear to her heart and is excited to share with others curious to unearth the secrets of Portland.

Jason Quigley is a self-taught freelance photographer. He learned just about everything he knows by photographing concerts and musician portraits, and he foolishly quit his engineering day job in 2013. He lives with his beautiful wife and two daughters in Southeast Portland, Oregon and thanks them profusely for their patience and support.